THE GENDERING OF
AMERICAN POLITICS

THE GENDERING OF AMERICAN POLITICS

Founding Mothers, Founding Fathers, and Political Patriarchy

Mark E. Kann

Westport, Connecticut
London

Library of Congress Cataloging-in-Publication Data

Kann, Mark E.
   The gendering of American politics : founding mothers, founding
   fathers, and political patriarchy / Mark E. Kann.
      p. cm.
   Includes bibliographical references and index.
   ISBN 0–275–96111–7 (alk. paper).—ISBN 0–275–96112–5 (pbk. :
   alk. paper)
   1. Sex role—Political aspects—United States—History—18th
   century. 2. Women's rights—United States—History—18th century.
   3. Political culture—United States—History—18th century.
   4. Patriarchy—United States—History—18th century. 5. Social
   role—United States—History—18th century. I. Title.
   HQ1075.5.U6K36   1999
   305.42′0973′09034—dc21   98–53397

British Library Cataloguing in Publication Data is available.

Library of Congress Catalog Card Number: 98–53397
ISBN: 0–275–96111–7
      0–275–96112–5 (pbk.)

First published in 1999

Praeger Publishers, 88 Post Road West, Westport, CT 06881
An imprint of Greenwood Publishing Group, Inc.
www.praeger.com

Printed in the United States of America

The paper used in this book complies with the
Permanent Paper Standard issued by the National
Information Standards Organization (Z39.48–1984).

10 9 8 7 6 5 4 3 2 1

For my students,

Who have filled my life

With great challenges

And even greater joys!

Contents

Preface

This book explores how America's founding mothers and founding fathers built gender biases into the very foundation of American politics. It examines traditional prejudices against women as well as efforts to overcome these prejudices during a revolutionary era. It inquires into the shifting male hierarchies that kept some men out of politics, admitted others on a limited basis, and privileged a few men regardless of the rhetoric of liberty and equality. It also assesses the enduring impact of the founders' gendered politics on modern America.

Fortunately, I have been able to draw on the marvelous research and writings of two generations of scholars who have studied women, men, and politics during the founding era (and beyond). Part of my motivation for writing this book was to make their findings and insights more accessible to students investigating gender and politics in America.

Many of the ideas and much of the analysis in this book grew out of research that I did for two previous books: *On the Man Question: Gender and Civic Virtue in America* and *A Republic of Men: The American Founders, Gendered Language, and Patriarchal Politics*. The strategy for organizing and writing this book grew out of my experiences as a classroom teacher who stressed a balanced focus on women and men, emphasized the often subtle but enduring effects of gender on American politics, and provided a concise summary of the major points at the end of each section.

I have acknowledged the help and support I have received from other scholars in my previous books. Here I wish to recognize the many, many students who have challenged me by their questions and comments to dig deeper into the gendered foundations of American politics. I also want to thank those students who forced me by their quizzical facial expressions to figure out ways to communicate ideas about the gendering of American politics with greater clarity, coherence, and cogency. Along with all of the other students who have made me smile, I dedicate this book to them.

I owe a special debt of gratitude to Tara Church, who was my undergraduate research assistant in the earlier stages of research and writing. Tara made an especially major contribution to Chapter 2. Furthermore, Tara's remarkable grasp and subtle reading of the works of writers such as Judith Sargent Murray added greater depth to the analysis throughout the book. Tara, thank you so much!

Finally, I must thank my family—for everything. Kathy and Simon, I love you.

INTRODUCTION

Founding Fathers and Founding Mothers

The Declaration of Independence expressed the American founders' belief that "all men" were born free and equal and could be governed only with their own consent. Did that mean that women were not born free and equal, and could be governed without their own consent? Did "all men" refer to all biological males or mainly to those males who measured up to contemporary standards of manhood? The founders' answers to these questions cemented gender bias into the foundation of American politics.

The American founders consisted of several generations of intellectuals, opinion makers, political activists, and public leaders. They were writers, orators, agitators, lawyers, ministers, magistrates, and statesmen who promoted protests against the British Parliament in the 1760s, led the struggle for independence in the 1770s, debated the merits of the U.S. Constitution in the 1780s, and then launched a new national government in the 1790s. They were mainly men—such as James Otis, Jr., Benjamin Franklin, Thomas Jefferson, John Adams, George Washington, and other lesser known figures. Some founders were women. Annis Boudinot Stockton, Abigail Adams, Mercy Otis

Warren, Judith Sargent Murray, and Susanna Rowson participated in the discussions and debates that helped to shape the
politics of the era.

Two crucial concerns for America's founding fathers and
founding mothers were to eradicate tyranny and to establish an
orderly republic. What did it mean to eradicate tyranny? By July
4, 1776, most colonial leaders identified the eradication of tyranny with gaining independence from British rule. Patriots
charged that King George III, his evil ministry, and a corrupt
Parliament denied Americans the natural rights of men, the historical rights of Englishmen, and the contractual rights in-
scribed in colonial charters. Overthrowing British rule would
open the way to "manly liberty." American revolutionaries demanded the manly freedom to exercise civil rights and to govern
themselves. Simultaneously, American men reaffirmed their
manly prerogative to rule their wives, daughters, and other female dependents. The peace treaty of 1783 symbolized patriots'
successful effort to champion men's liberty and perpetuate men's
domination of women.

The founders' commitment to manly liberty applied only to
some men. The founders did not consider a male fully qualified
for rights or citizenship unless he proved his manhood. In their
minds, a "real man" was an independent family man who fit into
society. He owned enough land to support a family. He married
a respectable woman and provisioned, protected, and governed
her. He sired sons and daughters to perpetuate his family dy-
nasty. And he cooperated with neighbors and contributed to the
community. The founders generally felt that only stable, substantial, settled family men had an unquestioned claim to citizenship. Other males (such as white paupers and enslaved
Africans) failed to measure up to manhood and could be excluded from citizenship.

What did it mean to establish an orderly republic? Part of the
founders' answer was to guarantee citizen rights, create representative political institutions, and implement checks and balances to neutralize factional conflict and prevent political corrup-

tion.* Part of their answer was to promote a republican culture that fostered among Americans a love of liberty, a respect for equality, an attachment to civility, and an enduring commitment to civic virtue—the willingness to engage in self-sacrifice for the public good. The founders felt that most citizens needed to exhibit some civic virtue to prompt them to defend liberty against its enemies and to exercise liberty with significant self-restraint.

From the first protests through the Revolution and beyond the Constitution, many founders feared that Americans were a disorderly people who exercised liberty without self-restraint. Large numbers of people used liberty as an excuse to pursue vices such as drinking, gambling, and promiscuity; to gain un-earned wealth through deception, exploitation, and robbery; to indulge greed through ostentation and luxury; to commit crimes and participate in mobs, rebellions, and mutinies against legitimate authority. Particularly during the years immediately following the Revolution, local and national leaders worried that Americans were transforming liberty into licentiousness and losing respect for virtuous and talented leaders. In private letters and public newspapers, the founders warned that people's disorderly conduct threatened the very survival of the new states and the national government.

Most founders were concerned with two categories of disorderly Americans. One category included all women, who were associated with public chaos. The founders saw women as lustful, fickle, selfish creatures. The best way to limit women's mischief was to subordinate them to fathers and husbands and to focus their energies on bearing and nurturing children. The most dangerous and disorderly women were those who sought to escape domesticity for social pleasure and political action. These "public women" jeopardized their own well-being and their families' welfare but also social peace and political order. Worse, they tempted "effeminate" men to engage in destructive pleasure-seeking and mob conduct. America's founding fathers and founding mothers overwhelmingly agreed that women's proper place was in the home and nursery where their vices and malicious influence could be restrained. They did not have to think twice about excluding women from public life.

The other category of disorderly Americans was composed of males who appeared to threaten public order. The founders associated young white libertines and all black males with lust, promiscuity, and rape; they identified vagrants, paupers, and backwoodsmen with lawless anarchy; they worried that lower-class men and even middling men harbored desires and jealousies that set them against substantial property holders and eminent leaders. Most founders were convinced that ordinary men had dangerous passions, impulses, and interests that threatened to subvert public order. Fortunately, most American men were sufficiently manly to settle into stable family life. They could be trusted with citizenship. Still, only a distinguished few men could be trusted with leadership.

Let me emphasize that the American founders spoke the language of liberty and equality but they simultaneously promoted the exclusion of women from politics and the subordination of most men to an elite male leadership. In one sense, then, the American Revolution, the U.S. Constitution, and the Bill of Rights changed very little in the public lives of Americans. Half of the population, women, did not gain new civil, political, or legal rights. Meanwhile, many men were no better off politically after the Revolution than before it. Poor men and itinerants continued to be disenfranchised; black men still suffered slavery and brutality; and Indian men were treated as barbarian outsiders. Even among white, propertied males who voted and sat on juries, there was a question as to whether the Revolution had really established a new republican order or simply an American version of Europe's highly centralized politics. In the 1790s, for example, some Americans felt that President George Washington was as powerful, if not more so, than any European king.

In another sense, the American founders promoted new ways by which women and men would understand politics. The founders helped to destabilize traditional gender relations by raising questions about whether tyrannical husbands were like tyrannical kings and whether women as well as men needed to consent to be governed. During the founding era, the lines separating feminine and masculine roles blurred and the revolutionary language of rights was applied to women—although it would be many decades before changing sex roles and revolutionary rhetoric resulted in the emergence of a movement for women's citizenship. Equally important, the founders helped to subvert the traditional politics of male preference and deference. Their revolutionary emphasis on liberty and equality raised public expectations about inclusive citizenship. Their use of democratic language spread across the American landscape and heightened people's hopes for greater popular participation in politics. Henceforth, neither the exclusion of women nor the subordination of large groups of men could be taken for granted.

The American founders left us a mixed legacy. They perpetuated gender bias and grafted it on to their new republic. They won a revolution and framed a constitution that excluded women from politics and subordinated large numbers of men to political elites. Patriarchy persisted. Simultaneously, the founders helped to weaken traditional gender biases and to disseminate a revolutionary rhetoric that would be used in later struggles to justify women's rights and democratic participation. In retrospect, America's founding fathers and founding mothers initiated a discussion and debate about the relationship between gender and politics that we continue to carry on today.

The Gendering of American Politics examines how the founders understood, altered, but ultimately affirmed women's political exclusion and most men's political subordination. It also investigates how they challenged traditional gender roles and political elitism. Part One focuses on common justifications for women's political exclusion, counterarguments intended to subvert male tyranny, and, finally, an informal compromise that admitted American women to a sort of second-class citizenship known as "republican womanhood." Part Two considers the founders' fears of disorderly men, their desire to legitimize the rule of a few heroic men, and, finally, an informal compromise that invited white family men to practice limited citizenship but reserved most political power for national elites. The Conclusion examines the evolution of the founders' gendering of American politics from their time to our time and into the twenty-first century.

PART ONE

Remember the Ladies

CHAPTER 1

Women's Exclusion from Politics

In 1776 Abigail Adams wrote to her husband John Adams that the delegates at the Continental Congress should "remember the ladies and be more generous and favorable to them than your ancestors." Abigail communicated two messages. One was that women should not be forgotten in the struggle for liberty. They had suffered the tyranny of men over women and they should be free from men's abusive rule. The other message was that women deserved greater respect and recognition than in the past. In particular, women should be treated as contributing members of society. They merited civic dignity if not actual citizenship.

The gendering of American politics began with the founders' forgetfulness. Most founders assumed that women were men's natural subordinates. They mostly forgot about women's rights and citizenship because they perceived politics as strictly a matter for men. The founders complemented their political amnesia with a disrespect for women's potential as independent persons and patriots. The revolutionaries who fought for the rights of men mostly scorned the idea of independent women contributing to the public good. They felt that any women who were not under the governance of men were dangerous, disorderly crea-

tures. The founders' forgetfulness and disrespect helped to perpetuate the *traditional patriarchy* that excluded women from
politics.

TRADITIONAL PATRIARCHY

The fact that men ruled women in early America received little attention. The practice of male domination and female subordination was traditional. It was embedded in the English laws
and customs that governed British Americans. Furthermore,
men's elevation over women was one of many hierarchies that
organized colonial society. Men governed women just as parents
ruled children, masters managed servants and slaves, teachers
exercised authority over students, gentlemen demanded deference from commoners, local elites controlled communities, and
kings exacted obedience from subjects. *Patriarchy*—men's
domination of women in family life, religion, culture, econom-
ics, society, and politics—was generally taken for granted. It received little consideration or comment.

Patriarchy was the organizing principle of family life. Parents,
ministers, and magistrates instructed young people that they
had a duty to marry and multiply. Sometimes parents arranged
pairings; increasingly, young people chose their own spouses.
Either way, the vast majority of young men and women consented to enter into a fixed marriage contract that granted a husband nearly absolute authority over his wife's body, behavior,
and property. A husband's authority was supported by the *law of
coverture,* which specified that a husband legally "covered" or
subsumed his wife's identity: he ruled her in private and spoke
for her in public. Ideally, a husband treated his wife as a partner
but, clearly, he was the senior partner. He governed family morality, managed family property and labor, and supervised children's upbringing and education as well as represented female
family members and other dependents in counting houses,
courts, and government offices.

The assumption of male dominance in families was so widespread that the founding generation did not consider challenging it. The power of kings and governors was questioned in the eighteenth century but coverture and related patriarchal laws would not be contested until the middle of the nineteenth century. It would be yet an additional century before Americans questioned a husband's legal control over his wife's body and demanded laws against wife battering and spousal rape. Historian Linda Kerber concludes, "It did not seem to have occurred to any male patriot to attack coverture."[1]

Because a wife was her husband's legal dependent, commentators presumed that she did not have an independent mind or independent will of her own. Her first loyalty was supposed to be to her husband. Ideally, *her* thoughts and deeds appropriately reflected *his* ideas and desires. Even a highly competent, intellectually astute wife who managed a large family, ran a complex household, farm, or business, and demonstrated mental talents and business acumen was not given much credit for individual intelligence or accomplishment. Mostly, she was appreciated as a "deputy husband"—a sort of temporary stand-in or substitute for the male head of her family.

Why would young women marry if their nuptials cost them recognition as autonomous thinking, acting human beings? Most early American writers argued that single women gladly exchanged their girlish freedom for lifelong love and companionship. Others offered the less romantic view that single women gave up independence in return for the promise of male economic support and the opportunity to bear legitimate children. Still others observed that single women who avoided marriage were likely to suffer humiliation. They were often stigmatized as sexually promiscuous, disorderly, deceitful girls and later as unfeminine, pitiful, even evil old maids. Popular novels regularly warned female readers to choose marital subordination to a husband rather than the coquette's self-destructive lifestyle or the spinster's barren existence.

Men's patriarchal domination of women pervaded America. It seemed natural and ordinary that husbands ruled their wives. The idea of male domination was deeply etched into men's identities as men. "Real men" exhibited self-control, productivity, independence, and civility by mastering "effeminate" vices such as impulsiveness, profligacy, and dependency. Males who failed to measure up to masculine norms were often disgraced by being identified with women. A soldier found guilty of cowardice might be court-martialed and then emasculated by being marched out of camp wearing a dress. Equally important, "real men" were husbands who ruled wives. Benjamin Franklin put it this way: "Every man that is really a man is master of his own family." He governed his wife with a firm but loving disposition and she responded with "a becoming obedience."[2] A husband who failed to control his wife was apt to be ridiculed by neighbors and held responsible for her misdeeds.

Sometimes men's domination of women was infused with *misogyny*—an outright hatred of women. Historian Kenneth Lockridge suggests that eighteenth-century American males suffered a deep psychological tension. On the one hand, they were attracted to women for sexual pleasure and they relied on women to give birth to their children. On the other hand, men feared being enslaved by women's seductiveness and sexuality. The resulting tension between attraction and fear gave rise to male sexual insecurity manifested in "patriarchal rage" against women. For example, the young Thomas Jefferson copied into his diary this nasty little verse: "Woman the fountain of all human Frailty! / What mighty ills have not been done by Woman? / . . . Who lost Marc Antony the World? A Woman. / Who was the cause of a long ten years War, / And laid at last old Troy in ashes? Woman. / Destructive, damnable, deceitful Woman!" Jefferson fantasized about a world in which men could live together in peace and reproduce without women.[3] These misogynist attitudes made it easy for men to believe that they should rule women.

The founders' misogyny was apparent in their language. Male intellectuals and politicians often defined politics as a manly struggle against dangerous female figures such as Fortune, Fancy, and Popularity. Thomas Paine depicted the American Revolution as the heroic effort of a maturing American male to free himself from a grasping British mother. He also described it as a conflict pitting American patriots defending manly liberty against corrupt British governors seeking to seduce Americans into female dependence. Many founders perceived the Revolution as a war between republican "manliness" and monarchical "femininity." If patriarchy meant that males ruled their families, patriarchal political rhetoric suggested that American males should govern the continent.

Most founders could not imagine a society where women were free and equal, and were governed by their own consent. They usually wrote and spoke about freedom, equality, and consent in politics as if women did not exist. One can read pages and pages of founding-era speeches, articles, and documents only to find little mention of women and even less interest in women's participation in politics. Generally, the founders took patriarchy for granted and forgot the ladies. Consider *The Federalist Papers*, the most important and famous defense of the U.S. Constitution. These popular essays spoke volumes about male intrigue, power, and politics but provided zero commentary on women's place in public life. Indeed, the authors' only references to women were a few mean-spirited remarks about female bigotry, petulance, and prostitution.

When a few founders did bring women into their political discussions, it was mostly to devalue them or to use them to make a point about men. Thomas Paine found women useful for propaganda purposes. He pointed out, for example, that "the whole race of prostitutes in New York were Tories" and also that Tories hatched treasonous schemes "in common bawdy-houses, assisted by those who keep them." Paine's point was to degrade prostitutes and then condemn Tories by associating them with prostitutes.[4] John Adams wrote briefly about women's exclu-

sion from voting rights, not to question it but to highlight
women's lack of qualifications and show why dependent men
also should be denied the vote. When political writers referred
to women, it was mainly to denounce them and men who
seemed to be like them.

On occasion, some founders explicitly expressed the need to
exclude women from public life. General George Washington
complained about female "camp followers" who traveled with
armies and provided important services to soldiers. He wanted
these otherwise helpful women isolated from his troops because, he believed, soldiering (as well as citizenship) was an exclusive male endeavor. John Adams openly opposed both the
female franchise and universal male voting rights. He wanted to
stem the rising tide of democracy to ensure that the common
mob was restrained and "the better sort" of men were entrusted
with political authority. Thomas Jefferson detested women's
participation in public affairs. He honored American women for
their domesticity and condemned French women for their disruptive influence in their nation's politics. Washington, Adams,
and Jefferson expressed these gender biases well before they assumed the reigns of presidential power.

The founders' forgetfulness about women, periodic diatribes
against them, and occasional pronouncements excluding them
from politics reinforced and perpetuated traditional patriarchy.
The founders were able to reinforce and perpetuate patriarchy at
the very same time that they promoted a revolutionary rhetoric
of liberty and equality because they shared five major justifications for male domination and female subordination that denied
women's participation in the nation's political affairs.

Justification One: Women's Domesticity

When questioning the authority of the British Parliament to
impose taxes on the colonies, American leaders began to reex-
amine the philosophical foundations of political obedience and
disobedience. They drew on the theories of Thomas Hobbes,

John Locke, and Jean-Jacques Rousseau to imagine a state of nature in which men were born free, equal, and rational. Even in a relatively tranquil state of nature, the theorists suggested, men's rights were insecure. A few vicious bullies threatened public order. Moreover, men did not have a forum for settling conflicts fairly and peacefully. These insecure men assembled, reasoned together, and consented to a social contract that organized society and set up a neutral government to protect men's rights and resolve their conflicts. The men who consented assumed the rights of citizenship, accepted the duty to obey legitimate government, but reserved the option to rebel against tyrannical governments.

Where did women fit into the story of the social contract? Most of the time, women were simply absent. For example, Samuel McClintock argued that a British attack on Massachusetts constituted an abuse of American rights and a betrayal of the social contract. Henceforth, "all the civil governments were dissolved, and the people reduced back to a state of nature, and in danger of falling into anarchy and confusion." Fortunately, "the people" organized themselves into "a band of brothers," created a voluntary "army of freemen," and consented to submit to their own government "for the safety of their country."[5] McClintock never took into account the possibility that "the people" included the many women ("a band of sisters"?) who participated in protests against Parliament, ran farms and shops when their husbands went to war, contributed to patriotic causes, and cooperated with America's makeshift governments. It was as if women did not exist.

Political analyst Carole Pateman suggests that women's place in public life went unnoticed because a "sexual contract" implicitly preceded the social contract.[6] The sexual contract was an informal agreement among men that women were different from and inferior to men. Women were maternal creatures whose proper sphere was domesticity. Their main purpose was to bear, nurse, and nurture children. Men were naturally stronger and more rational than women. Their main purpose was to sire children, provide food and shelter for their families, and protect them against enemies. In general, male thinkers assumed a sexual contract that required women to stay at home with their children while men forged a social contract, consented to government, and participated in politics.

Nearly all founders agreed that women were naturally suited for domesticity and that men alone were fit for public life. Thomas Paine vigorously denied any significant distinctions between aristocrats and commoners but he affirmed that natural differences between the sexes beckoned women to bear and rear children and obligated them to obey the men who provisioned and protected their families. John Adams succinctly summarized the founding generation's core conviction: "Nature has made [women] fittest for domestic cares."[7]

Most American writers were convinced that women's virtue and happiness were based on their cheerful willingness to render obedience to loving men as well as on their maternal desire to bear men's children. Parents, ministers, and popular culture told women that they could never be contented until settled into marriage and maternity. Writers praised mothers for procreating new generations of (male) citizens whose numbers strengthened the young nation; they criticized women who avoided marriage and maternity for reducing the nation's population growth and sapping its strength. According to a Benjamin Franklin satire, the only comparable threat to America's strength would have been if the British army sent a company of "sow-gelders" to castrate American men and thereby limit American population growth. The founders' common sense conviction was that women had to stay home and bear children if America was to survive and thrive.

Biology, religion, economy, and law reinforced female domesticity. Adult women endured constant pregnancies and multiple childbirths. Ministers enjoined wives to be fruitful and multiply. A farm economy situated amid abundant land rewarded large families. And husbands' legal right to their wives' bodies guaranteed constant impregnation. One consequence was that adult women regularly suffered physical disabilities associated with perpetual pregnancies and emotional traumas tied to miscarriages, stillbirths, and high infant mortality rates. Often maternity was so debilitating that women's participation in public life seemed to be implausible. The added expectation that women also were to be caretakers of the ill, disabled, and elderly made their participation in public life appear to be impossible.

Appearances were important. The time that a woman spent away from her domestic duties to engage in social activities or public affairs was often construed as a threat to her family's well-being. It was also interpreted as a sort of virus that infected other women and thereby endangered the family foundations of social stability and political order. Many Americans felt that women who sought to escape domesticity deserved disgrace and punishments that included self-inflicted guilt, husbands' discipline, social humiliation, and occasional legal action.

Other factors fueled the idea of female domesticity. An ideal *goodwife* was pious. She was expected to be a positive religious influence in her family. She cultivated a healthy relationship with God, exemplified religious devotion in daily life, taught piety to children, and encouraged it in her husband. Some founders felt pious women had such an immense impact on families that they could shape the morals and manners of the entire nation. Also, women's economic productivity strengthened their association with domesticity. A proper wife was a *helpmeet*. She manufactured household goods and clothing, tended animals and crops, perhaps took in boarders, and more. Her contributions to family finances were considered important enough to preclude her from investing time and energy in non-domestic matters such as public affairs.

Virtually all founders agreed that women who were occupied and fulfilled by their "natural" roles as wives, mothers, religious teachers, and economic contributors would voluntarily and happily submit to their husbands' authority. Even when they objected to aspects of their husbands' governance, they would obey to ensure family peace. By contrast, most founders felt that women who desired significant involvement in the marketplace or politics were likely to forsake their domestic duties and disrupt conjugal harmony. Theophilus Parsons did not doubt that women had the mental capacity to participate in the economy and politics, but he excluded women from public life because he believed they ought to occupy themselves with "various domestic duties."[8] The founders were committed to what they considered a natural division of labor that situated women in domesticity and made men the sole legitimate participants and decision makers in the economy and politics.

Justification Two: Women's Dependency

Virtually all founders assumed that women could not support themselves and their families or defend themselves, their families, and the nation against strangers, criminals, wayward soldiers, hostile Indians, and opposing European armies. Early American culture declared women to be naturally dependent on men for provision and protection. In turn, women's dependency on men precluded women from participation in politics and promoted men's domination of women in both private and public life.

Civic leaders demanded that men provide the basic necessities of food, shelter, and clothing for their wives and children. The common expectation was that a young American male would work hard to acquire land prior to marriage, farm the land to support his family during marriage, and accumulate a sufficient surplus to ensure that his daughters married well and his sons had enough land to marry, support their own families, and perpetuate the family line. In part, a young male proved his manhood by demonstrating his ability to head his own family, support female dependents, and provide a legacy for his male heirs.

Law and custom assisted him. A husband had legal control of virtually all family assets, including any property his wife brought into the marriage. He also managed family members' labor. In effect, he was the chief operating officer of the family firm. If his family was modestly successful, he was praised, respected, and trusted by his neighbors. If his family firm failed, he was likely to be condemned as a poor husband, father, and businessman and suffer emasculation, humiliation, and isolation from the community. Early America was a society where most business deals were based on men's word and mutual trust. Operating a successful family firm was crucial to men's reputation and economic prospects.

To the extent that men's reputation and economic prospects depended on their performances as family providers, any attempt to prevent men from supporting their families threatened their psychic manhood and social standing. That was part of the reason why Great Britain's pre-Revolution efforts to force accused colonists to stand trial in England aroused so much colonial anger. Sending a man away from home for prolonged periods deprived his family of their primary source of support and deprived the family man of his self-respect, reputation, and dignity. Relatedly, any attempt to enhance women's economic independence from their husbands threatened men's status as men and as family providers. With few exceptions, America's founding fathers and founding mothers rejected the emasculating idea that women should be free to achieve economic self-sufficiency. Husbands solicited wives' economic contribution but opposed women's material independence.

Similarly, husbands often solicited their wives' help to defend their families in times of peril, but they did not desire women to assume independent responsibility for protecting families or the nation. The founders assumed that women were not protectors. Their physical weakness, constant pregnancies, multiple childbirths, and physical disabilities along with their natural domesticity rendered them unfit soldiers. They were excluded from mandatory and voluntary military service. By contrast, men were protectors. All males between ages sixteen and sixty were expected to serve in militia units that maintained law and order and, in times of war, defended communities against enemies. The job of patriotic mothers, lovers, wives, and daughters was to urge their men to enlist and serve with courage. The job of male soldiers was to put themselves in harm's way to protect "beauty and booty"—female dependents and family estates—from rapacious enemy troops.

The founders often emphasized that men had to protect women from enemy seduction and rape. John Adams was angered by Tories who tempted girls into sin and then reproached them for it. He was incensed by the rapes committed by British troops stationed in Boston. Revolutionary pamphleteers such as Thomas Paine urged American men to fight to protect their women from the sexual violence of Red Coats and Hessian mercenaries. Popular novelists warned young girls against libertine deception, seduction, and rape. In Royall Tyler's play, *The Contrast*, several young women were being stalked by a rogue until Colonel Manly unmasked the rogue and banished him from society. A female character announced, "We each moment stand in need of a protector." The only "safe asylum a woman of delicacy can find is in the arms of a man of honor."[9] Seeking the protection of a man of honor meant marrying him and submitting to his patriarchal authority.

The commonplace conviction that women were dependent on men for provision and protection had a significant impact on how the founders understood politics. On the one hand, the founders believed that only independent people were capable of rational deliberation and participation in politics. As long as they viewed women as men's dependents, they would exclude women from politics. On the other hand, even when the rhetoric of rights was widespread, most founders felt that the truest marker of a person's loyalty to the nation was a demonstrable willingness to support families and defend the nation. In late eighteenth-century America, men alone had legitimate opportunities to be family providers and patriotic soldiers and, therefore, men alone could demonstrate that they deserved citizenship. Women were not recognized as providers or protectors (although they participated in both roles) and thus they were not even considered potential citizens.

Justification Three: Women's Passions

The founders saw women as especially sexual, passionate creatures whose powerful appetites and erratic impulses threatened to reduce men to slavery, transform liberty into licentiousness, destroy families, disrupt society, and subvert political order. Most founders figured that women's capacity for rational thought and reasoned behavior was quite limited but women's potential to abuse and corrupt public life was virtually unlimited. Ministers and magistrates more or less agreed that men monopolized reason and, therefore, only men merited citizenship.

Eighteenth-century writers often referred to women as "the Sex." This reflected their view that women were inherently impassioned creatures. Colonial culture often depicted women as sexual, seductive beings whose pursuit of pleasure extended from physical desire and coquetry through frivolity, fancy, and fickleness to deceit, witchcraft, malevolent power, and conquest. Allegedly, women lusted after every conceivable form of self-gratification. During and after the Revolution, the founders more commonly associated women with vices such as selfishness, material greed, unrestrained consumption, and an addiction to luxury. Seemingly all women—young maidens, middle-aged wives, and aged widows—were connected to cosmic forces that created chaos in the universe.

On the positive side, the founders felt that women's passions could be subdued by female virtues which included gentility, honesty, modesty, caring, loyalty, and piety. The problem, many writers suggested, was that women rarely subdued passions or practiced virtue on their own. Popular novels were filled with tales of "artless" females who were infatuated with libertines, deceived by them, and then abandoned by them to a life of shame, misery, and poverty if not suicide. The cultural rule of thumb was that impassioned young women needed sober male guidance in the form of paternal education and marital subordination. Ideally, parents schooled their daughters in female virtues that fortified their chastity and made them attractive to

prospective husbands. Once married, young wives were to submit to the guidance of husbands who had the authority to forbid
inappropriate behavior and encourage female virtues, maternal
responsibilities, and economic productivity. Properly schooled,
married, and governed by men, otherwise impassioned females
could become the moral center of family life.

The main explanation for why women needed to be governed
by men was that women rarely kept their passions within the
boundaries of reason. The founders gave several explanations
for female irrationality. One explanation was that women's
strong passions and weak reasoning powers were part of nature's
plan to propagate the species. A mother's love and partiality for
her offspring were useful passions for nurturing and protecting
babies through their infancy. Meanwhile, a father's rational disposition was needed to harmonize relations between the family
unit and the larger society. The implication was that women's
passions were suitable for the domestic sphere but inappropriate
in public life. That explains why in the 1790s Alexander Hamilton attacked Thomas Jefferson and James Madison for having a
"womanish" attachment to France. Hamilton echoed the basic
belief that female loyalties were fine at home but unreasonable
in politics.

Some writers suggested that women lacked men's intellectual
focus and depth. However, women still could benefit from a
practical education that helped them to protect their virtue and
contribute to their families. Women could be trained to recognize the nature of virtue and the necessity of practicing it. This
training would alert them to male deceptions, help them to
avoid seduction, guide them to choose worthy men as mates,
and show them why they should voluntarily obey their husbands. Women also could be taught improved domestic skills.
Benjamin Franklin praised the example of Dutch women who
learned accounting and business skills. Their frugal household
management and contributions to family finances were assets.
Importantly, they had the ability to safeguard family estates
when widowed. They could run family farms or shops until a son

came of age and took over the family business. The general idea that women should be educated to improve their domestic skills generated some skepticism but little serious opposition.

Far more controversial was the idea that women should have access to a similar if not an identical education to men's curricula. Some founders felt that women could develop their reasoning powers as well as men and might even exhibit a rational attachment to the public good. However, nearly all founders felt that educating women just like men was a serious mistake. Schooling women in the lessons of history or the practice of logic might "unsex" them. It would destroy female delicacy and modesty, weaken maternal instincts, and encourage abandonment of homes and family for pedantry and the professions. Most founders felt the prospect of a proliferation of independent, rational women was subversive of family life, destructive of social harmony, and disastrous for public order. Better that women cling to domesticity and allow men to provision and protect them.

Justification Four: Women's Disorders

The founders regularly depicted women as inherently promiscuous, deceitful, and dangerous persons—especially in public spaces. In Latin, "Publius," or a public man, was identified with civic virtue and patriotism. Americans believed that men who involved themselves in public affairs acquired a sense of civic dignity, a reputation for service, and even fame for contributing to the public good. By contrast, "Publica," or a public woman, was associated with prostitution and disruptive behavior. Many founders considered women who played out their powerful passions in public life as "disorderly women."[10] Their seductiveness, deceit, and scheming threatened the cause of national independence and then the survival of the new nation.

Topping the founders' list of female disorders was women's debilitating effect on men. Women epitomized temptation for men. Their animal magnetism encouraged men to neglect virtue and sink into vice. George Washington, Thomas Jefferson, Benjamin Franklin, and John Adams repeatedly warned the young males of their families and acquaintance to stay away from girls, strumpets, low women, and prostitutes lest they ruin their health, neglect their education, lose their wealth, engage in evil pastimes, and become accustomed to bad company. A young man needed to learn to resist women's sexual allure or risk life-long disaster. Worse yet, women were temptations to married men. Seductive coquettes, female prostitutes, loose servant girls, and accessible slave women proved to be irresistible to many husbands whose adulterous behavior, in turn, endangered family integrity and social stability. Finally, women were known for serving as messengers and spies whose sexual snares and deceitful airs tricked patriots into betraying their nation. The founders saw women in public streets or near military installations as destructive of manhood, citizenship, and nationhood.

High on the founders' list of women's disorders was their sheer selfishness and self-indulgence. The founders criticized domineering wives for emasculating their husbands; drunken wives for neglecting their families; and spendthrift wives for destroying family financial security. Popular guidebooks and magazines warned young husbands to control disorderly wives lest they and their children be victimized by them. On the other hand, wives who were fiercely devoted to their families were also dangerous to the public good. They urged their husbands and sons to neglect or evade their public duties. Revolutionary War leaders worried that mothers, wives, and lovers pressured men to stay at home when they should be marching off to war. Clinging women made recruitment difficult. They also undermined military campaigns by urging their men to demobilize or even desert their posts. General Washington constantly complained about troop shortages caused by recruitment difficulties, soldiers returning to their families, and deserters fleeing to their homes.

Many founders criticized disorderly women who engaged in what otherwise was considered virtuous behavior. Pious women who promoted religious revivals were sometimes condemned for displaying unruly religious passions that hinted at sexual promiscuity. Patriotic women who vehemently supported the Revolution were occasionally chastised for their aggressive attitudes and unruly behavior. During war, women who performed crucial services for soldiers were nonetheless reprimanded for slowing down the army or distracting soldiers from their duty as well as for stealing and spying. After the war, women with what appeared to be rational political concerns were apt to be blamed for manipulating male leaders or fostering corruption among them.

More so than most founders, Thomas Jefferson dwelled on disorderly women. He noted that his good-hearted male assistant "loses all power over himself and becomes almost frenzied" when in the company of women. Jefferson was against imposing harsh penalties on rapists lest disorderly women use the rape charge as "an instrument of vengeance against an inconstant lover and of disappointment to a rival." He condemned French women who engaged in public petitioning and protests for abandoning their families and nourishing "all our bad passions." He blamed France's Queen Marie Antoinette for an "inflexible perverseness and dauntless spirit," manipulation of the king, and the violence of the French Revolution. He commented, "I should have shut the Queen in a convent, putting harm out of her power."[11] Jefferson's misogynist tendency to blame women for all public problems was simply an extreme example of the founders' deep distrust of public women.

Not surprisingly, many founders joined fraternal organizations where men could escape from women to enjoy male camaraderie. Social groups like the Freemasons, martial institutions such as the Society of the Cincinnati, and political clubs like Democratic Societies were male-only organizations that invited members to congregate, socialize, network, deliberate, plan, and make decisions regarding their families, businesses, communities, and nation without women's presence, intervention, or interference. Indeed, the largest and most powerful fraternal organization in early America was the United States government, which was constituted by men, legitimized by men, and run by men. Women need not apply.

Justification Five: Women's Consent

American women were too constrained by childbearing, child rearing, caring for the sick and elderly, and other family responsibilities to devote much time to public life. Moreover, men's distrust of women's passions and disorderly behavior reinforced legal institutions and cultural norms that precluded women from participating in public life. Additionally, women were taught by parents and ministers and then prodded by husbands to be content with domesticity, resist any desires to engage in masculine pursuits, and accept politics as men's exclusive domain. Most founders believed that the vast majority of American women learned these lessons well, accepted conventional gender norms, and conceded men's political monopoly. That is, they believed that American women consented to men's traditional patriarchal rule.

Here again, Jefferson expressed an extreme version of common conviction. His diatribes against women who participated in the politics of the French Revolution were usually accompanied by hymns of praise to American women who gloried in domesticity and left political matters to their husbands. Jefferson condemned politicized French women as "Amazons" but applauded domesticated American women as "Angels." After all, American women were happy to accept "the tender and tranquil amusement of domestic life." They had the "good sense to value domestic happiness above all other." And they were "too wise to wrinkle their foreheads with politics." Their sole connection to public life was "to soothe and calm the minds of their husbands returning ruffled from political debate."[12] Like Jefferson, most founders felt that American women consented to this sexual division of labor.

American writers felt free to assume that women consented to men's political monopoly on another ground. Proper young ladies chose to marry. They agreed to wear "the hymenial chain." During the wedding ceremony, they consented to a fixed marriage contract that created a unified family unit in which husbands ruled their wives and spoke for their wives in public forums. Henceforth, wives were *indirectly* represented as part of a family unit when their husbands consented to the social contract, established government, and participated in it. Women's participation in the marriage contract and their indirect representation through their husbands constituted women's tacit consent to traditional patriarchy.

Most founders were convinced that women's consent to male rule was so natural and automatic that it was difficult to get women to speak publicly against their spouses or disagree publicly with them. Consider the issue of "dower rights." To prevent widows from having to rely on public assistance, legislators required husbands to reserve a portion of their estates—a dower—for their wives' support in the event of widowhood. A husband could not sell his wife's dower unless she consented to the sale. American officials assumed that a wife's obedience to her husband was so deeply ingrained that she would unthinkingly agree to anything her husband proposed, even the sale of her dower. Seeking to ensure that she fully understood and consented to any such sale, officials required that the wife be separated from her husband and interrogated in private so that she would feel free to ask questions and reveal her real choice.

Some founders felt that American women tacitly consented to men's political power whenever they expressed attachment to domesticity or showed appreciation for the *relatively* good treatment they received from American men. Jefferson praised America's white women for their commitment to family life. He believed they preferred marriage and motherhood to every imaginable option. He then noted that white women enjoyed "a sort of equality." They were respected as civilized beings capable of feminine sensibilities, and they were generally treated with respect by their husbands and children. Jefferson contrasted them to Indian women who, in his opinion, were treated as drudges

and draft animals. He concluded that white women surely consented to civilized "equality" over Indian women's more bestial
circumstances.[13]

The other side of the consent coin was that most founders
could not imagine that American women had any real objec-
tions to men's political monopoly. Americans inherited an English tradition that depicted women as childish creatures who had
little of consequence to say. Therefore, any views expressed by
women on important matters could be treated with little regard
or simply ignored. Consider Mary Fish Noyes' experience. When
she refused a suitor's marriage proposal, the rejected man wrote
to her father, "Sir, I do not, I cannot, I will not take your daughter's complaisant letter as a real, much less a decisive negative to
my proposal. I view it only in the light of female play, and have
taken the liberty to treat it accordingly."[14] Prolific writer Judith
Sargent Murray understood that being a women meant having
one's words discounted. That was why she published her major
works under a male pseudonym.

Men's disrespect for women's voices was especially strong in
public matters. For example, male judges and juries in early
American rape trials sometimes acquitted sexual predators despite positive proof that the female victim said "no" and explicitly denied her consent to sex. Indeed, male jurors and juries
often showed little interest in victims' testimony, especially
when they were low-status women such as servant girls or slaves.
Ultimately, men who refused to listen to women's voices or
heed them could assume women's consent to patriarchy and ignore any protests to the contrary.

CONCLUSION

The American founders did not invent patriarchal politics but
they perpetuated it by forgetting about women's contributions
and potential in public life and by showing little respect for
women's capacities as public persons. Their major justifications
for excluding women from politics were as follows:

1. Women were naturally suited for domesticity.

2. Women were not free and equal to men because they were dependent on men for provision and protection.

3. Women were passionate, irrational creatures who could not measure up to rational standards of citizenship.

4. Women were dangerous and disorderly creatures who threatened to destroy public order.

5. Women consented to patriarchy.

Assuming or stating these justifications, the founders applied the language of liberty, equality, and consent almost exclusively to men.

Nonetheless, most founders did feel that American women enjoyed "a sort of equality." American men honored women for their contributions to family life. Ideally, husbands showed wives respect and affection, solicited their cooperation and consent to family decisions, and ruled them with tenderness and mildness. Ideally, male citizens and political leaders cooperated to uphold men's rights to provision and protect their wives and children. Of course, the founders did not mistake ideals for reality as they saw it. And in 1776, for example, John Adams's version of reality was that nature declared women to be domestic creatures unqualified to carry on "the great businesses of life and the hardy enterprises of war as well as the arduous cares of state." He added that it was even dangerous to talk about political inclusiveness because the topic was "so fruitful a source of controversy and altercations."[15]

Of course, John Adams did talk about political inclusiveness if only to oppose it. He knew that the Revolution meant a partial suspension of women's subordination to men. During the war, the traditional boundaries between masculine and feminine roles blurred because everyone had to do whatever was necessary to ensure survival and achieve victory. And although many founders hoped to re-establish traditional patriarchy after the Revolution, others were less enthusiastic about men's behavior as rulers in both private and public life. Meanwhile, American women began to claim more authority in the domestic sphere and raise questions about men's political monopoly. We will see in the next chapter that some founders went so far as to challenge the major traditional justifications for men's patriarchal rule of women.

CHAPTER 2

The Case for Women's Inclusion

Young Thomas Jefferson's hatred for women reached back to the Biblical beginnings of humankind. He considered the following quotation about the Garden of Eden sufficiently insightful to copy into his diary:

> Destructive, damnable, deceitful Woman!
> Woman to Man, first as a blessing giv'n,
> When Innocence & Love were in their Prime;
> Happy a while in Paradise they lay,
> But quickly Woman long'd to go astray;
> Some foolish new Adventure needs must prove,
> And the first devil she saw, she chang'd her Love;
> To his Temptations lewdly, she inclin'd
> Her Soul & for an Apple damn'd Mankind.[1]

Jefferson's traditional, patriarchal reading of Original Sin blamed Eve for acting on malicious lust, causing Adam to sin and introducing misery into the world.

In 1790 Judith Sargent Murray published an essay entitled "On the Equality of the Sexes," which offered a different account of Eden. Murray portrayed Eve as a relatively innocent victim. She was deceived by a demon (pretending to be an angel) who appealed not to her passion but to her desire for knowledge. Adam was neither innocent nor deceived. He knew that Eve failed to attain intellectual perfection when she ate from the Tree of Knowledge. His motive to sin was mere "attachment to a woman!" Henceforth, Adam and his sons refused to admit responsibility for bringing evil into the world, falsely blamed women for it, and proceeded unjustly to degrade and dominate women.[2]

The fact that Murray could publish a challenge to the traditional, patriarchal reading of this Biblical story suggests that the dynamic changes of the revolutionary era had a discernible impact on how the founding generation understood gender and politics. Some founders did question the legitimacy of traditional patriarchy and criticize its major justifications. In the process, they developed a "pre-feminist" set of arguments and sensibilities that anticipated later movements for women's equality and citizenship.

QUESTIONING TRADITIONAL PATRIARCHY

Eighteenth-century America experienced major changes in gender norms within families. The traditional model of the stern patriarch ruling his family with an iron fist was gradually replaced by the modern ideal of the companionate marriage. Young men and women were increasingly free to choose their own mates. They expected romance and love as part of the marital package. They viewed marriage as a partnership founded on mutual respect and collaboration. And they saw parenting less as a father's prerogative than as a joint venture. Few Americans questioned the husband's status as family head but many people felt that he should govern with his wife, not over his wife. Americans who promoted marital cooperation often condemned abusive husbands as tyrants and praised solicitous husbands as enlightened men. This gradual movement toward greater gender equality in families prompted some people to ponder whether movement toward greater gender equality in society and politics was also warranted.

The gradual shift in gender norms revealed a gap between traditional patriarchy and actual practice. Although patriarchal laws and customs empowered men, American women were able to exercise influence over their own lives and over the men in their lives. Women's ability to accept or reject suitors, engage in or refuse premarital sex, grant or withhold affection from husbands, manage households, bear and raise children, contribute to the family economy, and, as widows, direct the disposition of men's estates and minor children provided women significant sway during courtship and marriage. Men had formal authority but women had informal and sometimes substantial leverage.

American women demonstrated that they could use that leverage, recruit allies, and create areas of female autonomy. Women used the power of social groups and the influence of gossip networks to control and punish men who misused patriarchal authority. They called on sympathetic ministers and magistrates to teach men greater respect toward women as well as to punish men who were physically and verbally abusive to women. Also, they engineered semi-autonomous spheres of public life and action that lay beyond men's immediate grasp or complete grasp. Women founded, participated in, and ran church organizations; they collaborated, socialized, and networked with female neighbors; and they established charitable societies— thereby assuming sovereignty over portions of the public world.

Women's ability to exercise power, claim rights, and govern parts of society helped to subvert traditional patriarchy by demonstrating that women could be independent agents of their own destinies rather than helpless dependents of men. Sometimes the mere perception of women as potentially powerful, competent people was enough to generate male rage and misogyny. Nonetheless, some founders recognized changes in gender relations, appreciated women's demonstrable competence, and showed a willingness to discuss women's potential individuality and rights, and even their political status. A debate topic at Yale

University in the 1770s was "Whether women ought to be admitted to partake in civil government dominions and sovereignty."[3]

This willingness to talk about female individuality, rights, and political status was animated by the founders' experiences with alternative models of womanhood. Traditional patriarchy was the English norm but everyday practice in early America was far more diverse. Many wives served as "deputy husbands" who managed farms, businesses, and dependents when husbands were away. Dutch women in the middle colonies as well as widowed women throughout America exercised considerable economic authority, engaged in legal proceedings, and achieved noteworthy successes without male supervision. Upper-class women, widows, and midwives often functioned as community opinion leaders, moral arbiters, and sought-after healers. Quaker, Baptist, and evangelical women wielded spiritual authority and held leadership positions in their churches. Native American women sometimes enjoyed considerable sexual freedom, control over agriculture, and political power. Enslaved African women asserted themselves through disobedience, rebellion, murder, escape, arson, theft, and feigned illness. Historically, American women have exercised substantial *de facto* power both in private matters and in public affairs.

The era's revolutionary language of liberty and equality lent some legitimacy to women's *de facto* power. The founders focused their rhetoric on "the rights of men" but their language suggested that all arbitrary authority wielded by one human being over another might be considered tyrannical. Accordingly, children challenged despotic parents. Students defied bullying professors. Apprentices confronted brutal masters. And abused wives stood up to tyrannical husbands. During an epoch when all human hierarchies were suspect, that most intimate hierarchy elevating men over women was also suspect.

Criticism of patriarchy was especially timely because women's participation in the Revolution blurred the conventional boundaries between men's roles and women's roles. Colonial women participated in economic boycotts and public protests.

When men went to war, their mothers and wives governed their families and dependents, ran farms and shops, made financial and marketing decisions, defended property and progeny from squatters, soldiers, and thieves, and demonstrated against price-gougers and profiteers. Patriot women also raised money and sent supplies to the military, cooked and washed for the troops, nursed sick and injured soldiers, and fought in combat. After the war, widows gained legal and political experience when litigating or petitioning on matters related to their fallen husbands' estates. War-time necessity forced women to exhibit their multifaceted talents. And women's effective exhibition was a powerful argument against men's claims to unilateral authority.

Women's growing influence in families, their *de facto* impact on society, their diverse relationships with men, their enthusiasm for liberty and equality, and their patriotic participation in the struggle for independence did not generate a national movement for sexual equality. However, these ideas and events did encourage some founding fathers and founding mothers to rethink traditional patriarchy in American society, question it, and develop pre-feminist criticisms of its major tenets.

EXPANDING DOMESTICITY

The founding generation assumed that women were meant to be men's wives and mothers of men's children. Within that context, however, some founders criticized the virtually unlimited extent of husbands' patriarchal authority over their wives. They also questioned whether women's domesticity necessarily prevented them from participating in social affairs and political matters. Critics of traditional patriarchy charged that domestic duties did not and should not keep women away from public life.

Eighteenth-century Americans increasingly complained about the powers that husbands wielded over their wives. A 1743 poem pointed to "a father's stern command" and then "the tyrant husband" as lifelong sources of women's "fatal bondage." A bit later, Grace Growden Galloway extracted this poetic lesson from her unhappy marriage: "Never get tied to a man / for when once you are yoked / Tis all a mere joke / of seeing your freedom again."[4] The rhetoric of the Revolution intensified criticism of husbands' abusive domination of their wives. Abigail Adams and Thomas Paine opposed the king's tyranny over Americans and then, by analogy, they also opposed men's long-standing tyranny over women. Their message was that husbands' authority needed to be restrained if women were to be treated as respectable, worthy human beings.

Why should women be treated as respectable, worthy human beings? A frequent argument was that women—like men—were moral, rational creatures. Annis Boudinot Stockton explained that "the Soul" had no sex. Indeed, female piety included "rational" virtues such as temperance, prudence, faith, and charity. Meanwhile, Mercy Otis Warren sought to correct men's mistaken belief in male superiority by arguing that women had the ability to equal men's achievements—even at "the most masculine heights." By the end of the eighteenth century, the conventional characterization of women as especially sexual, seductive creatures began to give way to the nineteenth-century portrait of women as asexual persons endowed with elevated moral understanding.[5]

This radical reassessment of female worth was accompanied by a growing conviction that women could fulfill their domestic duties as wives and mothers and then they could accomplish more. Judith Sargent Murray argued that women who ran their families also could give "mental attention" to intellectual reflection and imagination. They could achieve "every requisite in female economy" and then find the time to write down ideas or practice refined conversation. Murray wanted young women to be educated to be more thoughtful persons. Would educated women avoid or resent marriage? Not at all. Educated women "would become discreet, their judgments would be invigorated, and their partners for life being circumspectly chosen, an unhappy Hymen [marriage] would then be rare, as is now the reverse." An anonymous poet explicitly linked female education to conjugal happiness when she wrote, "Be generous then, and us to knowledge lead, / And happiness to you will sure succeed; / Then sacred Hymen shall in triumph reign, / And all be proud to wear his pleasing chain." Mercy Otis Warren added that educated wives comprehended and accepted female subordination "for the sake of order in families."[6]

Importantly, the cultural boundaries between domesticity and public life weakened during the founding era. The Revolution forced women to be both family providers and dedicated patriots. Women's effectiveness in public roles produced a sense of female competence that extended its reach from private life to the public sphere. For example, post-Revolution women transformed their traditional role as caretakers of children, the sick, and the elderly into the public role of caretakers of their communities. They founded, organized, and ran religious societies, benevolent institutions, and philanthropic drives to provide support for indigent war widows, orphaned children, and the needy. Women performed public functions that later would be assigned to the welfare state.

Recognition of female worth, rational virtue, elevated morality, education, and public participation did not emerge without challenge. In response to Abigail Adams's criticism of male tyranny, for example, John Adams complained about female tyranny. He avowed that men dare not repeal "our masculine systems" because patriarchy was men's only protection against the female seductiveness that threatened to enslave men and produce a "despotism of the petticoat."[7] Some champions of patriarchy complained that critics who wanted to limit husbands' authority were trying to emasculate men. Whenever a writer referred to women's elevated moral status, other writers were quick to respond with tales of female depravity, irrationality, and inferiority. Every time that women left home to attend school or participate in public life, they were vulnerable to accusations of dereliction of domestic duty and family desertion.

The post-Revolution debate about women's worth and place in public life was fueled by critics of traditional patriarchy who sought simultaneously to affirm women's natural domesticity and to recognize, enrich, and extend women's domestic talents into the public arena. It was now possible for at least some founders to imagine that female domesticity did not prevent women from public participation. Conceivably, one could be a wife, mother, worker, and citizen all at once.

LIMITED DEPENDENCY

Most Americans accepted as immutable fact that women depended on men for provision and protection. The concept of an "independent woman" was beyond consideration for most Americans and was positively subversive to others. Nonetheless, some founders began to question the degree of women's dependence on men and explore women's potential to become semi-autonomous individuals who took part in public affairs.

The War of Independence demonstrated that women could be competent providers for their families. For example, Abigail Adams was forced to take responsibility for her family's economic fortunes during the Revolution because her husband, John Adams, was away from home for years at a stretch. Abigail proved to be a remarkably successful entrepreneur in an unstable and unpredictable economy. She was more than a substitute for her husband; she was the primary family provider. One unmistakable war-time lesson was that women's traditional role as "deputy husbands" overlapped with men's responsibility as family providers. The idea that women should have access to a practical, business education to help them to sustain and improve if not manage family finances, especially during widowhood, became more widespread and acceptable.

Judith Sargent Murray noted that single women had long excelled in business. She offered numerous examples, including one that focused on a self-taught Massachusetts woman who developed a vast knowledge of agriculture, ran a profitable farm, and became a consultant to other growers. This businesswoman was a "complete *husbandwoman*" who led an independent, self-sufficient life. Her exemplary efforts contradicted prejudices about female dependency and weakness that were manifested in everyday labels such as "old maid" or "helpless widow." Murray believed that women should develop their business capabilities to the fullest extent possible.

She then went further than her contemporaries to argue that women should be educated for economic independence so that they could choose not to marry if they so desired. After making the usual arguments that a practical education would help women "to rescue many a family from destruction" brought on by men's dissipation and indebtedness, and that a practical education could prevent a new widow from becoming dependent on charity for her family's survival, Murray added, "The Sex [women] should be taught to depend on their own efforts for the procurement of an establishment in life." She believed that training all females for economic self-sufficiency would enable each young girl to "reverence" herself and develop her full capacities rather than "throw herself away" to the first man who flattered her vanity, promised to support her, and asked to marry her.[8] When defenders of traditional patriarchy complained that Murray's self-sufficient women posed a threat to manhood, family integrity, and public order, Murray responded that women who developed their economic capacities were still likely to decide to marry a male provider.

An important reason why many founders wanted to provide women access to a practical education and promote their contributions to family finances was that many men failed to be effective family providers. Popular advice books instructed young women that a husband's lack of sobriety, reason, competence, strength, and productivity might give a wife a right of governing in the family. Her challenge was to manage the family and provide for it but still keep up public appearances that her husband was the family provider and protector. Even Thomas Jefferson, no particular friend to women's rights and opportunities, recog-

nized the need to plan his daughter's education on the assumption that there was a fourteen to one chance that she would
marry a blockhead and end up having to manage and support
her own family.

The American Revolution provided evidence not only that
women could support their families but also that women could
be competent defenders of their families and the nation. Prior to
the Revolution, colonial women engaged in boycotts of British
goods and manufactured clothing and food substitutes for
banned British imports. They urged husbands, sons, and lovers
to join the protests and later the war, and they threatened to hu-
miliate reticent patriots by accusing them of unmanly behavior,
taking up the podium against them, and wielding weapons to
defend themselves regardless of them. Women's many-sided
participation in the war effort led to public expressions of respect for women's martial patriotism.

Throughout history, necessity has always urged women to
take up arms in defense of their families, estates, and communities. Benjamin Franklin noted, for example, that the colonial militia stockpiled paving stones between the windows of tall
houses. The stones were to be used by women "to throw down
upon the heads of any Indians that should attempt to force into
them." The early stages of the conflict with Great Britain indicated to some that American men might not be reliable defenders of liberty. In 1768 Milcah Martha Moore accused American
men of ignorance and cowardice because they failed to defend
liberty. Ten years later, on learning that the British occupied
Philadelphia without opposition, Abigail Adams declared, "If
men will not fight and defend their own particular spot, if they
will not drive the enemy from their doors, they deserve the slavery and subjection which awaits them." Where men would not
fight, American women took the initiative to defend themselves,
their children and farms, and their communities. Orators
praised women for their "manly exertions" against the Stamp
Act; applauded "female patriots" known as "the Daughters of
Liberty" for their protests against Britain; and honored female

defenders of families and farms during the war years. These heroic American women forgot female "timidity" and showed their "patriotic zeal."[9]

Thomas Paine evoked the image of Joan of Arc leading a dispirited army to triumph in the hope that "some Jersey maid [would] spirit up her countrymen and save her fair fellow sufferers from ravage and ravishment!" He praised women's military skills, although his main goal was to shame men into defending women against slavery and rape. If male patriots did not fight well, he warned, "they will see their homes turned into barracks and bawdy houses for Hessians, and a future race to provide for, whose fathers we shall doubt of." Judith Sargent Murray described a pantheon of heroic females to demonstrate women's positive potential for military valor. For example, Jane of Flanders protected her family and estate during her husband's imprisonment, organized supporters against foes, led warriors against a besieging enemy, and single-handedly fought her way through enemy lines to reach safety. Compared to most men, Murray argued, women were more capable of bearing hardship, as resourceful, unsurpassed in fortitude and heroism, equally brave, capable of supreme ardor, energetic, and loyal. Murray's goal was not to "array the Sex in martial habiliments" or "enlist our women as soldiers." Rather, she wanted Americans to recognize "the *capability* of the female mind" to equal any attainment within the reach of "*masculine exertion*."[10]

Some founders concluded that the common image of women as defenseless creatures was essentially false. Women could and often did play an expanded role, if not an independent role, in family provision and protection. However, most founders continued to give men primary responsibility for the family economy. They even perpetuated the belief that successful providers would be rewarded with "fat and frolicsome" wives. Furthermore, most founders (including founding mothers who supported greater sexual equality) believed that women ultimately were dependent on men for protection. Abigail Adams and Judith Sargent Murray called for greater equality between the sexes but expected men to be women's primary protectors. Still, the seed was sown that women had the potential for a greater degree of self-sufficiency. They could support their families, defend the nation, and exhibit the independence and patriotism associated with citizenship.

REASSESSING WOMEN'S PASSIONS

As the century wound down, respect for female morality and manners went up. Popular novels promoted the stock figure of the generous, devoted wife who forgave her errant husband for his adultery, gambling, and other male vices and then redeemed him to marital fidelity and moral virtue. Advice books called on women to inspire greater moral rectitude and good manners among all men. Educational writings emphasized the importance of exposing young males to the influence of righteous women. Noah Webster went so far as to assert that a young man's best defense against moral dissipation was "a fondness for the company and conversation of ladies of character."[11] Increasingly, the founding generation entertained the possibility that women were better than men at monitoring their passions and behaving with reasoned restraint.

A less radical but more common perception was that women and men were more or less the same when it came to indulging passions and controlling passions. George Washington's advice to his granddaughter was similar to his advice to his grandsons: "In the composition of the human frame there is a good deal of inflammable matter" which "when the torch is put to it . . . may burst into a blaze." Washington denied the idea that love was an irresistible passion. It was powerful but it could be and should be resisted by both girls and boys. Indeed, "love . . . ought to be under the guidance of reason, for although we cannot avoid first impressions, we may assuredly place them under guard."[12] Washington felt that both sexes suffered powerful passions but, fortunately, both sexes had the capacity to heed the voice of reason as a guide to good conduct.

Early American culture often stressed similarities between the sexes. Writers depicted both males and females as slaves to sexual lust and self-deception. They also described men and women as manipulative seductresses and malicious seducers whose vices ranged from lust and laziness to gambling and drinking. Simultaneously, writers affirmed that the sexes shared a capacity to restrain their passions with reason. Annis Boudinot Stockton claimed that women and men were "the same in mind" and Judith Sargent Murray declared "the equality of the female intellect to that of their brethren." Any differences between the sexes' reasoning ability were due to the fact that men monopolized educational resources. Why did men monopolize educational resources? Stockton claimed that men were envious of women whose natural wisdom enabled them easily to acquire "the spirit and strength of the masculine wit." Murray considered men selfish. They "usurped an unmanly and unfounded superiority" to sustain patriarchal power over women.[13]

Because both sexes were capable of "elevated understandings and the reverse," the isolation of women from educational resources had great significance. Untutored women suffered a low sense of self-worth, competence, and ambition whereas "learned ladies" were likely to excel at female virtues and accomplishments (without losing their feminine demeanor). Furthermore, if women's naiveté about society and the world made them vulnerable to "the snares of the artful betrayer," an important argument for female education was that it would provide women with sufficient wisdom to restrain their own desires while recognizing and repelling male schemers.[14]

Although late eighteenth-century Americans continued to perceive women as impassioned creatures, they were increasingly likely to assess women's passions as only mildly dangerous and disorderly when compared to men's ferocious passions. Women's lives were circumscribed by domesticity. Their vices had a limited reach. They mostly affected women themselves and their immediate families. By contrast, men's vices not only damaged and destroyed families; they also spread into the masculine sphere of culture, society, economy, and politics to wreak havoc there. Most founders were haunted by fears that men's passions, impulses, and avarice generated factional rivalries and public conflicts, subverted national economic order and development, and threatened to destroy republican government. The founders did not dwell on female passions, in part, because they were obsessed with controlling male passions. The most famous essay of the era was James Madison's Federalist Number 10, an extremely creative analysis about the best ways to subdue and neutralize male passions in politics.

The more that Americans were willing to grant women a capacity for self-control and reason (especially in comparison to men), the more they were willing to entertain possibilities for providing educational access to women. Judith Sargent Murray exalted women's capacity for reason. She wanted them to receive an education that would expand women's "fertile" brains and set free their "creative faculty." Formal schooling would strengthen female morality by fortifying women against temptation, seduction, and other detours from virtue; and it would encourage women to think in ways "worthy of rational beings." Ordinary wives would become superior companions whose virtue and wit would keep them attractive long after their physical beauty faded. Knowledgeable women would understand the dangers of luxury and promote the virtues of self-restraint and modesty against fad and fashion. Samuel Wales relied on the educated "daughters of America" to promote frugality, oppose luxury, and save the republic from men's greed, deceit, and base ambitions.[15]

Would education "unsex" women, make them act like men, and drive them to abandon domesticity—as defenders of patriarchy commonly suggested? Advocates of women's education claimed that female schooling would complement and reinforce domesticity. An educated young woman recognized the importance of family harmony and accepted subordination to her husband as the basis of family harmony. Annis Boudinot Stockton explained, "Women of the most exalted minds and the most improved understanding will be most likely to practice [the most] conciliating mode of conduct." Equally important, "men of sense" preferred learned women for their wives because knowledgeable women contributed to their families' well being and graciously accepted their subordinate status because they recognized its necessity.[16]

Judith Sargent Murray agreed that an educated woman made for a superior spouse but, as noted previously, she held open the possibility that educated women need not subordinate themselves to men. Conceivably, they could establish themselves "above that kind of dependency against which the freeborn mind naturally revolts."[17] Conceivably, they could emulate history's heroines who exemplified selfless patriotism and effective leadership. Conceivably, they could live up to republican standards of independence and self-reliance. Murray believed that men's claims to superiority were unfounded and she implied that educated women were qualified for public life, including political participation, citizenship, and statesmanship.

Many founders accepted and supported female access to higher education (but not an education for citizenship). Annis Boudinot Stockton was optimistic. In 1793 she wrote that "the empire of reason is not monopolized by men." In the decade since the Revolution was won, "great pains" had been taken "to improve women's minds." And fortunately, "we do not often see those efforts opposed by the other sex."[18] Less optimistic opponents to traditional patriarchy recognized that many civic leaders still suspected that education unsexed women, encouraged them to abandon their families, and tempted them to make claims to public power. Overall, most founders were willing to tolerate female education if it was situated in segregated academies that offered a specifically female curriculum intended to prepare girls to be better wives and mothers, not disorderly public activists.

ORDERLY WOMEN

Americans generally recognized that women had been important contributors to the struggle for independence. They had exhibited a capacity for self-sacrifice and patriotism in the service of the public good. Public recognition meant that women could not be perceived solely as disorderly creatures or as perpetual sources of public disorder. Instead, women were sometimes seen as exemplars of civic virtue and patriotic action. Did that mean that women were sufficiently trustworthy to merit political rights and citizenship in the new republic? Not quite.

During and after the Revolution, ministers and politicians praised American women for being patriots who urged fathers, brothers, lovers, husbands, and sons to enlist in the cause of liberty, prompted men to demonstrate courage under fire, memorialized those who died in battle, and rewarded worthy veterans with their esteem and affection. Orators regularly honored the mothers of heroic soldiers and statesmen for having procreated and educated the men who led patriots through the struggle for nationhood. Abigail Adams was one of many founding mothers who praised "learned women" for having reared "heroes, statesmen, and philosophers." And David Ramsay was one of many founding fathers who applauded "the patriotism of the ladies" when they parted with their husbands and sons and then exhorted them to exemplify courageous manhood in combat. Ramsay also heaped praise on those women who joined their husbands in combat, succored them on prison ships, and followed them when they were incarcerated in distant lands. Above all else, it was women's patriotism that animated men to risk "life and fortune in support of their liberties."[19]

No one debated whether American women defended families in ways that fostered the public good or made sacrifices for the public good. Annis Boudinot Stockton proclaimed, "I am no politician but I feel that I am a patriot and glory in the sensation." No friend to women in public life, George Washington accepted Stockton's distinction between patriotism and politics. He wrote to her that he certainly would not "rob the fairer sex of their share in the glory of a revolution so honorable to human nature for, indeed, I think you ladies are in the number of the best patriots America can boast."[20]

Americans occasionally transcended the traditional idea that women's main mode of patriotism was to motivate men to perform public service. Some founders suggested that women had their own, intimate stake in pursuing the public good. Hannah Webster Foster's fictional Mrs. Richman explained, "We [women] think ourselves interested in the welfare and prosperity of our country; and, consequently, claim the right of inquiring into those affairs, which may conduce to, or interfere with the common weal." Richman pleaded for women's place in public discourse. No, women did not expect to be "called to the senate or the field." However, women did "feel for the honor and safety of our friends and connections who are thus employed." Moreover, women's prospects were affected by public affairs: "If the community flourishes and enjoys health and freedom, shall we not share in the happy effects? If it be oppressed and disturbed, shall we not endure our proportion of the evil?" Women developed a strong emotional attachment to the public good. Accordingly, "the love of our country" was not "a masculine passion only."[21] The author's main point was that women's patriotism earned them the right to observe and discuss politics.

American women not only observed and discussed politics; some of them wrote about it, analyzed it, and staked out positions on it. Letter writing was considered an appropriate female endeavor. It provided elite women such as Abigail Adams and Mercy Otis Warren a medium for describing, discussing, and analyzing public affairs as well as for communicating their analyses to each other and to the powerful males in their social circle. Some American women published fictional and nonfictional writings filled with public observations and political advocacy in newspapers and magazines. Judith Sargent Murray's success as a magazine writer enabled her to publish a three-volume collection of essays entitled *The Gleaner*, which contained her most powerful statements on female equality. Her collection attracted 759 subscribers, including President John Adams, George and Martha Washington, and John Hancock along with other prominent politicians and literary figures.[22]

The idea that women deserved to participate in public discourse was partly based on the belief that women's domestic duties demanded that they take an interest in public affairs. Family women rightly worried about economic greed, moral decay, and political corruption in America. Vices such as drinking, gambling, profiteering, and criminality endangered their family finances; pastimes involving prostitution threatened their husbands' fidelity and their sons' innocence; and corrupt politicians imperiled their religions and churches. Women's domestic cares directed their attention to the marketplace, society, and government. Moreover, women of high morality and good manners were taught to care about welfare issues that affected family members, relatives, friends, neighbors, and the larger human family. For them, domesticity was an admission ticket into political deliberations.

Some founders went so far as to suggest that women's moral impact on the economy, society, and politics could be decisive. For example, Joseph Lathrop called on women to help make "industry" reputable in America. When female "vivacity, strength, and activity" were no longer considered "too indelicate, coarse, and masculine for a fine lady," he argued, more and more women would chose honest work over corrupting luxury. In turn, their example would promote industry among America's lazy, spendthrift men. George Washington also called on women to serve the public. Specifically, he wanted American women to help build a greater sense of national solidarity in the new republic. Shortly after the U.S. Constitution was ratified, he called on American women to promote "federal fashions and national manners" to unify diverse Americans and promote the "good morals and good habits" conducive to good government.[23]

Certainly, many founders were unmoved by women's contributions to the nation. They still saw women essentially as disorderly creatures. But many founders praised women's virtues, recognized their influence over men, and pondered their potentially positive impact on public life. If women's war-time patriotism could be transformed into peace-time devotion to good morals, productivity, and unity, it was conceivable that women could be seen as public-spirited patriots and contributors to the public good rather than as dangerous and disorderly influences on public affairs.

WOMEN'S DISSENT

Did American women dissent against men's patriarchal rule? Clearly, some founders *began* to imagine alternatives to patriarchy. In the 1760s James Otis, Jr., expressed the possibility that women had as much right as men to participate in the social contract, vote in elections, and represent themselves in government. A decade later, Abigail Adams raised the issue of whether women had a right to consent, take part in elections, and share political power. However, the vast majority of founders never considered replacing patriarchal politics with women's equality and citizenship.

Thomas Paine was typical of the most radical male founders. He recognized men's tendency to tyrannize over women. But rather than defend women's civil and political rights, he merely suggested that men should show greater respect for women. Modern scholars debate whether Abigail Adams shared Paine's position. She agreed that men had been tyrannical to women and should be more respectful to them, for example, by giving up "the harsh title of master for the more tender and endearing one of friend." Scholars' question is whether Adams was being serious or ironic when she declared that we women "will not hold ourselves bound by any laws in which we have no voice or representation."[24] Regardless, neither Adams nor other American advocates for greater sexual equality explicitly advocated the right of women to citizenship. Founding mothers such as Annis Boudinot Stockton, Mercy Otis Warren, and Judith Sargent Murray agreed that relatively independent, educated, competent, active womanhood was nevertheless consistent with women's *political* subordination.

One might argue that most American women even consented
to their political subordination. First, they consented when they
signed a marriage contract which gave to their husbands legal
control of their bodies, behavior, property, and children. Married women agreed to allow their husbands to govern them and
to speak for them. Additionally, American women consented by
default when they demanded greater respect within families,
more economic independence, better educational opportunities, and recognition for their patriotism but did not demand the
political rights and citizenship that might subvert patriarchal
government. American women expressed little desire to claim
political equality and citizenship. And without encountering a
forceful claim, most founders readily assumed women's tacit
consent to the continuation of patriarchal elections, governments, and laws.

Nonetheless, some early Americans began to imagine that a
woman might lay claim to the same political rights and prerogatives of male citizens. Some founders began to question rather
than take for granted women's exclusion from politics. For example, James Wilson explicitly asked why women did not share
men's political power. He granted that women were as virtuous,
honest, and wise as men. He even named great historical women
with equal if not superior military and political ability to men.
He concluded, however, that women were "made for something better" than public life and that something better was
"domestic society" where "the lovely and accomplished woman
shines with superior lustre."[25]

Historian Linda Kerber argues that the idea of female citizenship was increasingly conceivable to Americans though still un-
acceptable to them. In the 1805 case of *Martin v. Massachusetts*,
the court had to decide whether a women necessarily submitted
to her husband's choice to favor or oppose the Revolution, or
whether she could claim to be a competent citizen who was able
to think, speak, act, and make political decisions about revolutionary loyalties on her own. The court "found it impossible to
imagine adult women as anything other than wives and ruled

that a woman was obligated by her husband's political decisions." However, the woman's attorneys were able to make the argument that men and women should be seen as independent people, that husbands and wives each could evaluate the Revolution and other public issues for themselves, and that women's ability and responsibility for making public decisions constituted their "civic capacity."[26] That the lawyers could speak of women as persons with a civic capacity signified that at least some Americans displayed a pre-feminist capacity to challenge the idea that politics was strictly a patriarchal endeavor.

One might argue that some early American women indirectly dissented against political patriarchy. Subtly, they indicated they were not contented with their subordinate status and they did not consent, explicitly or tacitly, to be governed by men. Their protests against men's tyranny within families, their active public roles during the Revolution, their publications promoting greater sexual equality, and their analyses of post-Revolution political events all suggested that a small but critical mass of America's founding mothers did appreciate female political capacities, sought gradually to weaken the rule of both family patriarchs and patriarchal politicians, and hoped thereby to hasten the day when women's full citizenship was not only thinkable but recognized as justifiable.[27]

CONCLUSION

The founders' traditional justifications for patriarchal politics were destabilized during the founding era. Their major justifications for excluding women from politics were undermined by pre-feminist counterarguments that provided a more positive picture of women's private and public potential. The main counterarguments were:

1. Women's domesticity was a basis for women's moral elevation and public participation.
2. Women were able providers and protectors, exhibiting the independence and patriotism essential to citizenship.

3. Women's passions and reason refined by education made them as trustworthy as men in private and public life.

4. Women's capacity for morality and proven patriotism made them contributors to public order.

5. Women mostly consented to patriarchal politics, but they also questioned it in ways that anticipated female citizenship.

Following this reasoning, some founders sought to admit women into public life but without allowing them full citizenship.

The founders faced a dilemma. On the one hand, changing gender relations in families, a growing sense of female capacity and power, recognition of alternative gender relations, revolutionary language, and women's patriotism during the Revolution significantly undermined the legitimacy of the conventional assumptions about the justice of political patriarchy. Domesticity had expansive possibilities. Women showed themselves capable of provision and protection. They exhibited elevated morality and comparable rationality to men. And they practiced a patriotism essential to the defense of liberty. Women deserved an important role in the new republic. On the other hand, powerful factors worked against admitting women to political equality and citizenship. Men resisted changing families, female empowerment and education, and women's rights and political influence. Ultimately, many founders appreciated women's contributions to their families and the nation, but they were not ready to trust women to act independently in politics.

The founders had four options for resolving the tension between their devotion to traditional political patriarchy and their emerging recognition of women's public potential. One option was to recognize patriarchy, smooth over its rough edges, and make female subordination more palatable. Henceforth, greater emphasis would be put on what John Dickinson called "the mild features of patriarchal government" in which father figures directed matters important to the whole family but allowed female dependents a limited degree of autonomy and a greater degree of public respect.[28]

A second option was to highlight the gap between revolutionary America's democratic ideals and its refusal to treat women as men's equals. Eventually, Americans would recognize the need to close the gap. Abigail Adams repeatedly reminded her husband that male leaders had failed to recognize women's political potential. She ended one letter with this sarcastic remark: "As [politics] is a prerogative to which your sex lay an almost exclusive claim, I shall quit the subject."[29] Change would have to be gradual.

The third option was to subvert patriarchal norms by arguing for women's educational and economic opportunities, which eventually would strengthen women's case for full citizenship. Thus, Judith Sargent Murray promoted a vision of female autonomy, individualism, and economic self-sufficiency that would become the foundation for nineteenth-century demands for women's political power. Women's freedom, education, and productivity would demonstrate that women were as qualified as men to vote, sit on juries, and hold public office.

Fourth, some founders sought to infuse women's domesticity with intense political meaning. Women's roles as the wives of citizens and mothers of future citizens were given new prominence in the 1780s and 1790s. Some founders felt that female influence on male family members was the single-most important determinant of the nation's future. They gradually developed the doctrine of "republican womanhood," which called on domestic women to take responsibility for breeding, teaching, and sustaining good citizenship in America. We will see in the next chapter that this union of domesticity and politics constituted a key compromise in the gendering of American politics during the founding era.

CHAPTER 3

The Doctrine of Republican Womanhood

Educator-novelist Susanna Rowson described women as "that sex whose morals and conduct have so powerful an influence on mankind in general."[1] Rowson spoke for the many founders who believed that women's grasp on men's hearts was a potent source of female influence. Women could use their feminine charms and domestic leverage to exercise informal authority over their husbands and sons as well as over their culture, community, nation, and world. The key question was whether women's influence would be used for good or for evil. The American founders gradually developed a doctrine of "republican womanhood" that urged wives and mothers to use their influence to improve the nation's morals and manners and to promote among men the civic virtue and good citizenship essential to the new republic.

FAMILIES AND POLITICS

Traditional patriarchal marriages involved practices such as parents arranging marriages for their children, husbands ruling their households with unquestioned authority, and fathers using corporal punishment to discipline children. A new republican family ideal emerged in the late eighteenth century. It depicted marriage as the voluntary choice of partners seeking mutual affection, a union based on spousal cooperation, and a joint parenting endeavor that replaced physical punishment with the psychological use of praise and shame. Bridget Richardson Fletcher described the new marital ideal in poetic terms: "Would man and wife, live free from strife, / How happy might they be, / If they would try, in harmony, / To live in unity."[2]

The new ideal was still patriarchal. Men retained ultimate authority to make decisions within marriages and to represent families in society, the marketplace, and politics. However, the new ideal counseled that male authority should be restrained and held in reserve to ensure that mutual affection, cooperation, and consent among husbands and wives served as the basis for everyday decision making. The most important everyday decisions concerned child rearing. Popular literature advised fathers and mothers to work together to raise virtuous children by rewarding good behavior with affection and punishing misconduct with shame or humiliation. The goal of the new parenting strategy was not simply to discipline youngsters; it was also to shape children's attitudes, make their good conduct habitual, win their gratitude, and earn their enduring consent to parental and public authority.

A writer calling herself a "Matrimonial Republican" was exceptional. She went beyond calling for restraints on men's power over women. She wanted to eliminate men's marital superiority altogether. She proclaimed, "I object to the word *obey* in the marriage service because it is a general word, without limitations or definition. . . . The obedience between man and wife, I conceive, is, or ought to be mutual. Marriage ought never to be considered as a contract between a superior and an inferior, but a reciprocal union of interest, an implied partnership of interests, where all differences are accommodated by conference."[3] Few founding fathers or founding mothers went this far. Most founders perpetuated patriarchal authority within families but also sought to temper it.

Commentators hoped that husbands and wives who lived up to the new ideal would exemplify and transmit to their children "family values" such as voluntarism, affection, cooperation, and consent. Importantly, these family values were the same virtues that most founders associated with citizenship. Good citizens appreciated liberty as the foundation for voluntary choice and, when necessary, they took up arms to defend it. This commitment to liberty and its defense fostered among men a sense of mutual affection and shared commitment to the public good. Citizens bound together by affection and commitment were likely to sacrifice self-interest, exhibit civic virtue, cooperate to achieve the public good, and consent to obey their chosen governors. In summary, many founders believed that those families that approximated the new ideal were seedbeds for good citizenship and models of republican harmony.

Given widespread beliefs about women's natural domesticity, many Americans thought that women played an especially important role in promoting the family values conducive to good citizenship. Women's emotional influence on males, their association with piety and morality, their willingness to engage in self-sacrifice for others, their central role in nursing and nurturing infants, and their informal leverage as household managers and deputy husbands positioned them to have a profound impact on male norms, conduct, and habits. As men's lovers, betrothed, and wives, women had the potential power to reclaim males from vice by seducing them to virtue. They could use their sexuality, their economic roles, and their influence in church and civic organizations to subdue men's selfishness, encourage male rectitude, foster family responsibility, and deepen citizen virtue. Conceivably, women's positive influence could neutralize men's tendencies toward disorderly behavior.

Leading male founders regularly admitted that they personally depended on their wives to keep them on the path of virtue and good behavior. For example, Benjamin Rush anticipated that his marriage to Julia Stockton would check "the impetuosity of youth" and "regulate the ambition of manhood" as well as eventually prevent "the avarice of age." Rush planned to rely on his new wife to guide him toward a life of "piety and usefulness" and rouse him "to new exertions of patriotism." Similarly, Alexander Hamilton counted on his new wife to help him avoid temptation and do his civic duty. Shortly after marrying Elizabeth Schuyler, Hamilton confessed that he was so smitten with his bride that he wanted to spend all of his time with her—only to neglect his public responsibilities. He asked Elizabeth to reproach him "for an unmanly surrender . . . to love" and teach him that her esteem was "the price of my acting well my part as a member of society." Benjamin Franklin capsulized the founders' common sense when he observed that good wives made good husbands and good husbands made useful citizens.[4]

Estimates of women's ability to transform flawed men into good husbands and useful citizens were magnified by women's role as mothers of today's boys and tomorrow's men. Mothers could instill in their sons the predispositions, values, knowledge, and skills that prepared them for lives of adult piety, civility, patriotism, and public service. Mothers' pedagogical authority grew as America became more commercial and industrial. Fathers increasingly left their homes for separate workplaces and mothers were left with primary responsibility for raising children. Parenting manuals began to address mothers more than fathers. They gradually gave mothers precedence in parenting and anticipated the nineteenth-century belief that "*mothers alone*" could transform male infants into moral adults and good citizens.[5]

Simultaneously, mothering seemed to become more complex. Parenting was no longer a simple matter of instilling obedience into children or training them in specific skills. In particular, Americans perceived parenting sons as a difficult challenge aimed at developing a boy's conscience, moral character, and capacity for self-government so that he could assume the rights of men without abusing them, prosper in a fluctuating economy, grow his own branch of the family tree, and fulfill his citizenship responsibilities. Gendered assumptions about women's domesticity and men's breadwinning duties translated

into the conviction that mothers were the only parents with sufficient time, commitment, and virtue to transmit good character
to their sons and help them mature into devoted family men, responsible providers, trustworthy patriots, and future statesmen.
Thus, the founders often called on American women to practice
"republican womanhood" by calming their husbands' passions
and guiding them toward good citizenship, and by raising their
sons to be moral men and law-abiding citizens.

Most founders felt that women's informal influence over
their husbands and sons was immense regardless of patriarchal
laws and traditional customs that perpetuated men's formal
authority over women. In rural America the boundaries between masculine and feminine roles were ill-defined because all
family members had to work the family farm. Women's identification with religion, their contributions to family finances, and
their primacy in child rearing positioned them to be republican
women who shaped their husbands' and sons' conduct. Although the cultural boundaries between masculine and feminine were more distinct in urban areas, perceived gender
differences sometimes heightened women's influence. Urban
wives assumed *de facto* control of their households when their
husbands left home for separate workplaces. Occasionally, they
stretched their domestic influence into local churches and communities, for example, to protest against prostitution, gambling, and drinking establishments that lured their husbands
and sons away from virtuous manhood and good citizenship.

The American Revolution, the U.S. Constitution, and the
Bill of Rights did not bring independence to American women.
Nor did these landmark political phenomena enhance women's
economic opportunities or admit women to citizenship. Patriarchy persisted. The immediate result of the founding of the
United States of America was the perpetuation of what historian
Joan Hoff calls "a masculine system of justice."[6] Nonetheless,
the intellectual ferment and historical events of the era did influence the founders' conception of women as potential political
creatures. The doctrine of republican womanhood suggested

that wives and mothers were strategically positioned to shape the future of American politics. Women were crucial influences on the men of the republic. Their ability to mold male morals and manners would determine if virtue and harmony would predominate, if citizens would be trustworthy and patriotic, and if national leaders would be able to establish and maintain an orderly polity. Did American women have the capacity to assume and fulfill these political responsibilities?

EDUCATING REPUBLICAN WOMEN

The doctrine of republican womanhood acknowledged women's war-time contributions, enlisted wives and mothers in the service of the nation, and then justified female education by providing a clear domestic purpose for it: women should be educated to guide their husbands and train their sons to be good citizens. Many founders felt that women were fully as educable as men. Mercy Otis Warren stated that "human nature [is] the same in both sexes." Novelist William Hill Brown noted that "the female mind is competent to any task."[7] Even founders who doubted women's capacity for intellectual understanding felt that most women could benefit from formal lessons in domesticity. Gradually, the early American debate shifted from whether women should have access to schooling to what was the appropriate focus and content of female education.

Specifying the appropriate focus and content of female education could be a complicated matter. On the one hand, revolutionary rhetoric suggested that women should be educated for independence. They should learn to discipline their passions, elevate their reason, make conscientious decisions, develop economic skills, cultivate civic virtue, and practice patriotic loyalty to the nation—just like men. On the other hand, prevailing patriarchal prejudices suggested that women's learning should be confined to narrowly defined domestic skills such as husband-pleasing, housekeeping, and child rearing. Women should be schooled to be better wives and mothers. Many founders staked

out a middle ground. They wanted women to develop independent minds but they also wanted women voluntarily to
choose to live within the confines of domesticity.

In late eighteenth-century America, the traditional upper-
class practice of educating women to be marriageable fashion
plates was giving way to the republican notion that women
should cultivate reason, benevolence, and skill. Education reformers argued that schools ought to teach women to develop a
sense of competence and confidence that would enable them to
make self-conscious, rational decisions about their future as well
as to understand and withstand the inevitable adversities in life
that threatened their future. A significant portion of female education should aim at cultivating attitudes and abilities that
strengthened women's sense of character and competence
along with their knowledge. This suggested that reformers
wanted female education to approximate male curricula that
also emphasized character, competence, and knowledge.

Most founders were uncomfortable with the idea of offering
similar curricula to female and male students. Would women
educated like men also want manly independence? Would they
desert their families, assume masculine traits, and invade men's
sphere? Would they threaten men's authority within families and
men's monopoly in politics? Reformers responded by denying
that an education for independence would unsex women, drive
them from their families, challenge men's dominance at home,
or generate disorder in public life. Their argument was quite the
opposite. A learned lady understood that pride in domesticity
and obedience to one's husband were necessary and desirable. A
learned lady recognized that men and women had separate
spheres even though "it takes equal powers of mind and understanding properly to fulfill the duties . . . marked out for us—as it
does for the other sex."[8] Moreover, a learned lady was likely to
attract a learned husband who had high ideas of women's rationality and appreciation for women's application of intelligence to conjugal happiness.

Reformers also claimed that educated women usually were better mothers. They assumed greater responsibility for procreating and raising not just sons and citizens but also leaders. One graduate of a Susanna Rowson's female academy stated, "A woman who is skilled in every useful art, who practices every domestic virtue . . . may, by her precept and example, inspire her brothers, her husband, or her sons, with such a love of virtue, such just ideas of the true value of civil liberty . . . that future heroes and statesmen, who arrive at the summit of military or political fame, shall *exaltingly declare, it is to my mother I owe this elevation.*"[9] Ironically, many founders felt, women should not be educated for citizenship because they had an even more important task: to breed and mold tomorrow's (male) citizens and leaders.

The founders generally believed that America desperately needed trustworthy citizens and leaders. Indeed, it needed heroes and saviors who could lead the nation against vice, defend liberty, achieve prosperity, and hold off hostile powers. More than a few founders felt that America's future depended on the emergence of a few great women who procreated, reared, and educated a few great generals who would manage national security as well as a few great statesmen who would govern the young nation and fulfill its divine destiny in the world.

Alice Izard did not doubt that a divine force had established sexual differences that ought to be reflected in education if America was to achieve its destiny. She wrote, "The great author of nature has stamped a different character on each sex, that character ought to be cultivated in a distinct manner to make each equally useful, and equally amiable." For almost all founders, female education was not about developing independent women. It was about fostering women's distinctive capacity to guide men toward worthy pursuits and guard them against destructive temptations.[10] Ultimately, women were not to be political participants or politicians but men's political guides and guardians.

POLITICAL GUIDES AND GUARDIANS

If women were to guide men to civic virtue and guard them against political vice, their education would have to include a strong public focus. Some founders argued that women needed to study moral principles and political practices in order to encourage greater virtue and patriotism in their husbands and teach mature manhood and good citizenship to their sons. Equally important, women needed to develop a sense of political efficacy. They had to feel confident that their domestic actions would have a substantial, positive effect on public life. Ideally, republican wives and mothers armed with political knowledge and self-confidence would consciously and proudly transform their homes into schools for good citizenship.

Within the context of traditional patriarchy, positive images of female domesticity and dependency were usually accompanied by negative images of female passions and disorders. Leaders believed that women needed to be confined to their homes where men could govern them and prevent them from making public mischief. The doctrine of republican womanhood signified an important change. It linked positive images of female domesticity and dependency to positive estimations of women's capacity to enrich public life by educating and influencing male citizens. Many founders felt that American women were capable of forgoing past associations with frivolity, fashion, and fickleness in order to study political history, examine public affairs, deliberate on important issues, and commit themselves to pedagogical responsibilities that connected family life to important political matters.

Republican women who sought to keep men virtuous, teach boys civic virtue, and motivate husbands and sons to defend liberty would be most effective if they developed a sound understanding of public life and fully appreciated their family stake in the public good. Some founders argued that women especially needed to learn about the fragility of liberty if they were to take the initiative to alert their husbands and sons to threats to liberty and then encourage their men to petition, protest, and even take up arms to protect liberty. An important subtheme in colonial protests and the Revolution was that educated women's commitment to liberty, their insights into its imperiled status, and their awareness of its enemies were essential for awakening American males from their "unmanly slumbers" and rousing them to patriotic action. This was a compelling example of how women's political knowledge affected men's citizenship.

Some founders felt that women needed to study political history to better understand liberty and related public matters. By revisiting the past, they would learn about "the vices and follies of the human heart" that endangered people's liberty, threatened tyranny, and caused the downfall of republics. By investigating the history of other nations, they would be alerted especially to the dangers of "luxury," which fostered selfishness, destroyed virtue, generated self-destructive conflict, and brought disorder to society. In turn, women's sensitivity to luxury would allow them to identify and combat the key vices that threatened the peace of post-revolutionary America and made the nation vulnerable to internal conflicts and external enemies.[11]

In addition, politically knowledgeable women could guide and guard the nation by extending domestic norms into the public world. In particular, they could serve as caretakers of public piety and morality. Historian Joanna Bowen Gillespie writes that women's "religious rhetoric . . . furnished the vocabulary of citizenship." Just as ministers often identified the good Christian with the good citizen, republican women could identify family values with civic virtue and good citizenship. Also, they could transform social gossip networks into instruments to enforce religious beliefs and public morals. And they could protect their families and the public from passionate, impulsive, and greedy men by engaging in the politics of protest. Abigail Adams reported to John Adams, for example, that a hundred women had seized a price-gouging merchant, opened his warehouse, and distributed his goods. John's half-serious, half-joking response was, "It seems the women of Boston begin to think themselves able to serve their country."[12]

Knowledgeable women who claimed moral responsibility for their families and the nation had the capacity to extend ideas of female domesticity into once-exclusive male arenas. Mercy Otis Warren researched, wrote, and published a major three-volume history of the American Revolution. She recognized that it was the "peculiar province of masculine strength" to record history but gave four reasons why she need not yield "to the assertion that all political attentions lay out of the road of female life." First, domesticity afforded her time to observe, analyze, and write the story of national independence, whereas "every manly arm" was occupied on the battlefield or in politics. Second, Warren had a domestic stake in telling the story because she was connected by blood and friendship to leading patriots. Third, she argued that "every domestic enjoyment depends on the unimpaired possession of civil and religious liberty" and, therefore, she had a domestic duty to tell the story of Americans' defense of liberty. Fourth, proclaiming that "the welfare of society ought equally to glow in every human breast," her own concern for the nation's welfare was sufficient reason for her to write the Revolution's history. Warren molded domesticity into a justification for subverting conventional gender distinctions and allowing women to enter into the nation's political conversation.[13]

Did the doctrine of republican womanhood invite women to grasp formal citizenship, including the right to vote, sit on juries, serve in the militia, and hold public office? At times, Americans recognized and appreciated patriotic women for their efforts on behalf of liberty. Often, leaders recruited women to join the postwar struggle against vices such as avarice, swearing, gambling, drinking, whoring, and criminal activity that seemed to threaten newborn liberty. Taken together, women's patriotic past and contemporary connection to civic virtue made it at least thinkable that they had the potential to be more then men's guides and guardians; perhaps they could become full-fledged citizens.

Judith Sargent Murray came closer than any eighteenth-century American to linking republican womanhood to citizenship. She was confident about women's capacity to contribute to the public good. After all, women were equal to men not only in intelligence but also in political virtues such as fortitude, bravery, fidelity, patriotism, even heroism. Her main reservation concerned whether American women had enough ambition to reach beyond their households to have a direct impact on their communities, the nation, and the world. Hoping to inspire American women to make a political difference, Murray researched and disseminated stories of outstanding public women who had exhibited civic virtue and acted with great effect in Western history. For example, she told the story of Zenobia, Queen of Palmyria, who united valor and genius and "governed with rectitude, firmness, and intrepidity." She used this story and others to convince American women that they were capable of "any attainment," including political discussion, participation, and governance.[14] Nonetheless, Murray was a product of her times; she did not explicitly call for full citizenship for women.

Overall, then, the doctrine of republican womanhood provided women an informal avenue of legitimate influence in public life but it still did not justify formal female citizenship. Most founders simply could not imagine women claiming citizenship. It was one thing for republican women to influence their husbands and sons, talk and write about politics, and even engage in moral reform efforts. But it was quite another thing to suppose that women could cast votes, wield weapons, or govern men. America's founding fathers and founding mothers almost never talked about providing women direct access to political authority.

THE POWER OF EDUCATED WOMEN

Reformers were enthusiastic about the power of educated women to improve male morality, neutralize male misconduct, and enhance male citizenship and leadership. They saw educated women as the main cure for disorderly male behavior and public disorders. Refined young ladies who were sufficiently wise to reject the advances of deceitful libertines but welcome the honorable affections of virtuous, patriotic young men could revolutionize society. Their rejections would drive young men away from sin and their affections would lure young men to virtue. The grand result, according to Benjamin Rush, was that young men would be "restrained from vice by the terror of being banished from [female] company" and young men would be driven to virtue—even undertaking "the hero's dangers and the patriot's toils"—to win women's "approbation." In an America where young women were taught virtue, exhibited it, and demanded it from their men, the nation's stability and happiness were virtually guaranteed.[15]

Reformers also felt that educated women who became wives and mothers were particularly well positioned to promote benevolence, respect, and responsibility as well as to restrain unruly passions, impulses, and avarice among their husbands and sons. Most founders considered a virtuous wife and prudent mother to be the foundation and inspiration for the "great or good men" whose patriotism promoted the public good. Educated mothers were especially important because they were the earliest and most powerful influence on boys. They made the first impressions which were considered the most lasting impressions. Ideally, educated mothers promoted cordiality in families, softened "the savage rudeness" of their boys, ingrained in them "such sentiments of virtue, propriety, and dignity as are suited to the freedom of our governments," and directly instructed them "in the principles of liberty and government."[16] Women's positive pedagogical influence meant that men and boys would be more apt to act with restraint, foster social harmony, and obey the law.

The founders commonly believed that educated women—those who Noah Webster called "females of worth"—were the main motivation for men to be good citizens. It was "the fair daughters of America" who urged men to defend liberty and promised their respect and love to "men of character." It was the exemplary "patriotism of the ladies" that animated men to be courageous in the defense of liberty, risk their lives and fortunes for their families, endure great personal sacrifices and hardships, and withstand the innumerable sufferings of war. Precisely because educated women could transform disorderly men into patriotic citizens and good soldiers, the founders often saw them as the nation's best hope for securing political stability and martial solidarity. Simeon Doggett claimed that educated women even had the capacity "to fix the boundaries of human improvement" and "reform the world."[17]

While women's role as men's moral guides, guardians, and stabilizing agents was somewhat traditional, it achieved heightened importance in the new republic. Most founders felt that American men had to exhibit civility and civic virtue for the new nation to endure and flourish. Where men had great freedom, they needed to treat each other with respect and tolerance in order to prevent small disagreements from escalating into factional conflicts and national conflagrations. Where the political system was founded on consent rather than coercion, men needed to be willing to resolve most disagreements through discussion and engage in some self-sacrifice for the public good. Accordingly, educated women who guided men toward civility and civic virtue performed a profound public duty: they encouraged men to be trustworthy citizens.

After the Revolution, two factors increased the importance of women's stabilizing role. First, civic leaders feared that America was experiencing an epidemic of male vice and crime. Particularly in urban areas, male vagrants, paupers, thieves, rapists, murderers, and other criminals seemed to grow in numbers and destructive influence. Benjamin Rush in Pennsylvania and Thomas Jefferson in Virginia started to rethink the nature of crime and punishment. They supported building new-style prisons called "penitentiaries" intended to deter crime and punish criminals but also rehabilitate them to their families and good citizenship. Educated women were allies in the deterrence and rehabilitation process. Their encouragement of virtuous, law-abiding behavior helped to prevent crime and their commitment to men's moral reclamation helped to reform criminals. For many founders, educated women were an integral part of the solution to the problem of disorderly men.

Second, many founders feared that postwar America experienced an explosion of material greed that threatened to undermine the public good. They complained that men's selfishness, scheming, gambling, and speculation had replaced revolutionary-era feelings of solidarity, fraternity, and patriotism. They also feared that men's materialism and their obsessive pursuit of "self-interest" would create chaos in society and foster factional conflict in politics. Fortunately, republican women had the potential to resist male selfishness by teaching husbands and sons the virtue of self-restraint, the need to make sacrifices for their families, and the importance of recognizing their family stake in community harmony and national stability. Educated women excelled at the virtues that counteracted men's most common vices.

At a time when men appeared to recognize few restraints, women's stabilizing influence was thought to be especially important. The founders believed that women could temper men's passions, restrain their impulses, and direct their interests toward their families and communities. Women could guide men toward piety and morality as well as encourage them to cultivate civic virtue and good citizenship. Indeed, part of the reason that many founders began to accept men's self-interested behavior in the marketplace and their factionalism in politics was because they simultaneously relied on women to restrain men's excessive greed, encourage their good behavior, and guide them toward a degree of public-spiritedness. Great expectations that women could cure men's worst excesses gradually "allowed the unsentimental, self-improving, restlessly ambitious, free, and independent man to hold sway as a universal hero."[18]

The founders discussed republican womanhood as if it were "a fourth branch of government."[19] They hoped that men's

:nsus on values such as individual liberty and political
c͟ ality would support national unity. They engineered innovative political institutions to neutralize men's passions and check
their excesses. Equally important, they relied on educated
women to be America's guardians of men's civic morality. From
within their families, women could counteract men's criminal
tendencies and reduce their greed while encouraging their law-
ful behavior and patriotic practices. Educated women could
make a crucial contribution to public life despite their exclusion
from citizenship.

CONCLUSION

The doctrine of republican womanhood promised to reconcile female domesticity with public service in the following ways.

1. A new marital ideal invested republican women with public significance. They could transform husbands and sons into virtuous men
   and good citizens.
2. Republican women needed access to an education that promoted a
   capacity for independence but perpetuated a preference for domesticity.
3. Republican women needed to develop a sense of political understanding and competence to guide husbands and sons to civic virtue
   and guard them against public vice.
4. Republican women were powerful enough to counteract men's
   criminal tendencies, reduce their greed, and motivate them to be
   liberty-loving soldiers and law-abiding citizens.

Many founders were willing to accept, even applaud, women's
influence, education, participation in political discussions, public writings and analyses, and efforts at moral reform in exchange
for women's contributions to taming disorderly men and stabilizing republican society. Still, the founders did not invite
women to assume citizenship. They perpetuated government as
men's patriarchal preserve.

Let me emphasize that the doctrine of republican woman-hood promised limited public influence for women. First, the doctrine focused almost exclusively on privileged white women. Abigail Adams, Mercy Otis Warren, and Judith Sargent Murray were fortunate to be able to afford the leisure and expense entailed by a life of learning and scholarship. These founding mothers had a special sense of political efficacy because they moved among very influential men. For them, it was quite conceivable that women's influence on fathers and sons could have a substantial impact on public life. By contrast, artisans' wives, farmers' daughters, and slave women had little access to education and less reason to believe they were raising heroes and statesmen. The doctrine of republican motherhood had little meaning for most American women.

Second, republican womanhood still restricted women to a domestic sphere that was ruled by men. Husbands retained legal authority over their wives and local magistrates retained the power to detain disorderly women. The result was that women could exercise some influence over their husbands and their communities but only insofar as powerful men were open to female influence. Jan Lewis reminds us that republican women's influence was contingent "upon masculine susceptibility." Furthermore, nearly all founders agreed that republican women remained dependent on men and subordinate to them. Judith Sargent Murray promoted equality between the sexes but she too admitted women's dependency: "We confess that the superiority is indubitably yours; you are by nature formed for our protectors."[20] The founders continued to see even influential, educated republican women as men's economic, legal, and political subordinates.

Third, the doctrine of republican womanhood implicitly promised to pacify disorderly women. Women who were busy guiding their husbands and sons or learning to be better wives and mothers were unlikely to have the time or desire to engage in independent, impassioned behavior. However, the doctrine of republican womanhood did provide women a relatively safe outlet for their political passions. Women's legitimate "political activism" focused on their families and, by extension, on the morals and manners of their communities. Importantly, it did not focus on a battle for women's rights or a struggle for women's participation in politics. As historian Carol Berkin notes, "Full political participation was never an option."[21]

Fourth, arguably, the doctrine of republican womanhood was less about women than about men. The founders wanted to ensure order among women and the doctrine declared that women had important work to do that would pacify them and enable them to contribute to the public good. However, the founders were much more concerned with ensuring order among men. They were obsessed with the "man question": Were American men too unruly to be trustworthy citizens of a republic? Republican womanhood provided part of the answer. The founders recruited wives and mothers to tame men's passions, temper their exercise of liberty, and encourage law-abiding citizenship.

The gendering of American politics began as a compromise between traditional patriarchal ideals (Chapter 1) that subordinated women to male authority and emerging republican norms (Chapter 2) that recognized women's capacity for independence, reason, and patriotism. The compromise was manifested in the doctrine of republican womanhood (Chapter 3), which perpetuated women's exclusion from full citizenship but provided women sufficient educational opportunity and political influence to raise and educate the citizens and leaders of the new republic.

One result of this compromise was that an enduring gender bias was etched into the foundation of American politics. The founders portrayed women as residents of the domestic sphere. First and foremost, they were wives, mothers, and caretakers. These domestic roles necessarily colored perceptions of their actual or possible place in politics. For the most forward-looking founders, women's greatest political contribution was to serve as wives and mothers who transformed husbands and sons into law-abiding citizens. Women's secondary contribution was to extend domestic virtues into local communities by providing religious, welfare, and philanthropic services to neighbors in need. With the partial exception of Judith Sargent Murray, America's founding fathers and founding mothers could not imagine rights-bearing women exercising citizens' choices or political leaders' prerogatives.

Henceforth, women who claimed the same civil and political rights as men—or even suggested that such a claim was justifiable—were likely to be labeled doubly dangerous. Women who claimed public rights stood accused of neglecting if not forsaking domesticity. These allegedly neglectful women were vulnerable to blame for everything from men's political corruption to boys' criminality. Next, women who claimed the rights of men and sought release from patriarchal restraints were likely to stand accused of acting on irrational passions, impulses, and avarice. These so-called disorderly women might be blamed for everything from family ruin to national insecurity. In Chapter 7 I will consider how the ongoing association of women with domesticity still shapes the practice of American politics today.

Let me conclude Part I by pointing out that the founders justified for women a limited, indirect form of political influence. Many writers were quite sincere when they proclaimed that women's domestic influence had the potential to change the nation and world. In retrospect, however, I believe that it is fair to suggest that the more closely women were bound to domesticity, the more difficult it was for them to extricate themselves from it to achieve political equality with men.

PART TWO

The Ranks of Men

CHAPTER 4

Disorderly Men

Why did the founders rely on women to reclaim their husbands from vice and instruct their sons in virtue? The founders feared that most males were disorderly creatures. They indulged their passions, acted impulsively, and engaged in greed at the expense of other people and the public good. When Abigail Adams asked John to "remember the ladies," John joked about rebellious women but expressed grave concerns about unruly men. The Revolution had "loosened the bonds of government everywhere." Boys disobeyed parents. Apprentices defied masters. Students were turbulent. Indians rejected white guardians. Slaves were insolent to owners. Adams and other founders feared that conflict in the ranks of men was escalating into massive public disorder.

How could leaders prevent public disorder? The founders developed two main strategies. First, they effectively excluded from citizenship males whose "effeminate" behavior indicated an inability to discipline desire and act orderly. Second, they sought to reform disorderly men. The founders relied on cultural norms and social pressure to get young men to settle into stable marriages, assume family responsibilities, and be civilized by republican women. They also supported using public humiliation and political coercion to rehabilitate males who engaged in licentious conduct and criminal behavior. These strategies employed the dominant standards of manhood to justify exclusion and motivate reform.

THE DOMINANT STANDARDS OF MANHOOD

The meaning of manhood was complex in late eighteenth-century America. The traditional ideal of the manly landowner, stern family patriarch, and devoted citizen-soldier was challenged by emerging images of the sociable republican farmer and artisan, the refined middle-class gentleman, and the aggressive entrepreneur. Meanwhile, many founders doubted that enslaved African males had any claims to manhood and most founders were ambivalent about Indian males' masculinity. A libertine subculture in urban areas made matters murkier. It linked manly reputation to social vice and female degradation. This complexity notwithstanding, nearly all founders agreed on a few dominant standards of manhood.

How did a boy become a man? Most important, he needed to show that he could be an independent person. He had to discipline his passions, check his impulses, and restrain his greed if he was to avoid being enslaved by the darker side of human nature. The main means for him to exercise such self-discipline was to consult his reason and virtue and use them to guide his conduct. Once a boy demonstrated that he really could control himself, he was likely to win the respect of most older males. In effect, then, a boy stepped onto the pathway to manhood by observing, developing, and exhibiting what the founders referred to as manly integrity.

Equally important, a young male established his independence by achieving a degree of economic self-sufficiency. He worked hard and long to acquire the skills and resources necessary, ultimately, to own his own farm or shop. Once he became self-employed (and employed others), he was in a position to determine the nature and pace of his own labor. He could keep himself free of other men's patronage and government relief. He could refuse to be bought by wealthier men. His modest prosperity enabled him to exercise his own free will and fortified him to resist external pressure. A man who controlled his own economic destiny could stand up to powerful opponents and eventually stand for the public good.

What did a maturing young man do with his personal and economic independence? He invested it in family life. Popular writers and novelists characterized bachelors as slaves to sex, money, fad, and fashion. By contrast, they portrayed married men as sober, trustworthy persons. Young men who chose to become husbands and fathers explicitly agreed to provision and protect their loved ones. They made their lives more fulfilling and meaningful by perpetuating their family lines. Their commitment to the welfare of wives, children, and future progeny provided them a lasting stake in social stability and the public good. Most founders felt that family men were unlikely to behave in disorderly ways if only because their loved ones were likely to suffer the consequences of their misconduct. Marriage settled down otherwise disorderly young men.

Newly married men faced a crucial challenge. Commentators warned that enamored young husbands were apt to lose their independence to seductive and domineering wives. Critics regularly ridiculed the stock figure of the henpecked husband. Accordingly, part of young men's maturing process was to transform themselves into manly husbands who governed their wives rather than unmanly husbands who were ruled by their wives. Mature men knew how to govern their wives lovingly but firmly. They could be warm and affectionate. They could solicit their wives' advice and consent. But they were still authoritative family patriarchs.

Most Americans expected the mature family patriarch to fit into respectable society. A mature male not only exhibited personal integrity, family responsibility, and authority over women. He also cultivated *civility*—the art of getting along with other men. A well-bred young man seized every opportunity to serve and oblige his neighbors. He practiced politeness and even mild flattery to conciliate other men rather than to alienate them. In a changing society where liberty gave men considerable freedom to disagree, the founders considered civility to be a master virtue because it contributed to mutual tolerance, social peace, and public order.

George Washington epitomized civility. As a child, he copied one hundred ten "Rules of Civility and Decent Behavior in Company and Conversation" to help him become "manful, not sinful." Washington sought to maintain a "manful" reputation throughout his life. As a soldier, he tried to walk "in such a line as will give the most general satisfaction." In his farewell address to the Continental army, he challenged demobilizing soldiers to "carry into civil society the most conciliating dispositions."[1] Men who exhibited civility could disagree with each other but still trust each other, cooperate with each other, and share the rights and responsibilities of citizenship.

The founders agreed that mature, trustworthy (white) males demanded, defended, and deserved the "rights of men," including rights to life, liberty, property, and the pursuit of happiness. These mature men were free to negotiate a social contract to protect their rights, consent to civil society, constitute new governments, and participate in politics by deliberating on important issues, voting in elections, sitting on juries, and serving in militia units. Ultimately, these mature men were "procreative" men. They not only sired infants to perpetuate their family names and family lines; they also gave birth to infant republics to perpetuate their immortal renown.

To summarize, the founding generation believed that boys needed to establish independence, assume family responsibilities, govern women and other dependents, fit into civil society, and practice citizenship to achieve mature manhood. Those males who achieved maturation deserved to savor a sense of individual pride, social respectability, and civic dignity. They felt like men and were usually respected as men.

Notice that these dominant standards did not include stereo-typical characteristics such as sexual conquest or aggressive competition. The founders regularly criticized libertines who built their reputations by conquering the chastity of innocent girls. They often censured entrepreneurs, speculators, and gamblers who profited from other men's misfortunes. The founders consistently emphasized those standards of manhood that were likely to ease rather than foster disorder in the ranks of men.

Notice also that the dominant standards of manhood stood in opposition to *traditional* images of womanhood. The founders saw mature men as independent persons but depicted women as dependents. They endowed husbands with the responsibility to provision, protect, and govern families but associated women with maternity and subordination. They praised family men who exhibited civility and citizenship but warned against female incursions into public life. In effect, mature men were "not-women." This definition reinforced men's patriarchal rule over women by linking the meaning of manhood to female subjection. It also suggested that immature men were something less than men; they were "womanish" or "effeminate." This was important. A male who was considered more woman than man had a questionable claim to the rights of man.

EFFEMINATE MEN

In 1766 Reverend Jonathan Mayhew congratulated American men for defending colonial liberty by protesting against the British Stamp Act. Then, in an about-face, he criticized colonial men for transforming liberty into license. Many American protesters engaged in "riotous and felonious proceedings" and "rapacious violences." They produced a "state of general disorder approaching so near to anarchy" that they nearly brought on "more dreadful scenes of blood and slaughter."[2] For the next four decades, the American founders were haunted by the specter of men engaging in crime and rioting, inviting anarchy, and promoting violence.

Most founders felt that a basic part of the problem was that so many men failed to measure up to the dominant standards of manhood. They lacked the self-discipline, virtue, and reason of independent men. They refused to fulfill the responsibilities of family men. They did not behave with civility to their neighbors. And they spoke the language of civic virtue without practicing it. Often, they were slaves to their own passions. Often, they pursued self-destructive and socially destructive pleasures. Often, their egomaniacal pursuits worsened social conflict and political disorder. Many founders felt that most American men were immature. Hurling perhaps the greatest insult at them, national leaders asserted that common men acted *just like women*!

Why were American men so apt to act *just like women*? The founders' most frequent explanation was that men had an abstract capacity for measuring up to the dominant standards of manhood but they regularly failed to develop that capacity or act on it. Instead, they engaged in passionate, lustful, impulsive, greedy, and erratic pleasuring-seeking behavior. Benjamin Franklin wrote about men's penchant for self-indulgent vice and disorderly conduct in a satire about "Celia Single," who sought to set straight the public record in this letter to the editor:

I have several times in your paper seen severe reflections upon us women for idleness and extravagance, but I do not remember to have once seen [criticisms of] men. . . . I could furnish you with instances enough. I might mention Mr. Billiard who spends more than he earns at the green table . . . Mr. Finikin who has seven different suits of fine clothes . . . while his wife and children sit at home half naked . . . Mr. Crownhim who is always dreaming over the checkerboard . . . Mr. T'Otherpot the tavern-hunter. . . .[3]

Franklin spent a good part of a lifetime criticizing and satirizing men who practiced womanish vices. Thomas Jefferson even entertained the idea that, overall, men were more enslaved by passion and ignorance than women.

Another one of the founders' explanations for men's tendency toward disruptive behavior was that traditional restraints

on male conduct were rapidly disappearing. After the first protests against Parliament, defiance to authority increased dra-
matically. American men became enthusiasts for individual
liberty against established authority. Many founders worried
that American men were too enthusiastic. They used liberty as
an excuse to indulge their selfish desires regardless of everyday
morality, legitimate laws, and dangerous consequences. Many
men engaged in crime and collective violence. John Adams detested "private mobs" and the "rude and insolent rabble." General Washington was outraged when his soldiers rioted and
refused to respect "proper authority."[4] Civic leaders worried
that American men did not respect any authority.

John Adams believed that American men's demands for liberty became so excessive that their willingness to exercise manly
self-restraint in their private conduct and obey legitimate leaders
in public life was highly doubtful. Adams feared that most
American men not only refused to obey their own legitimate,
elected authorities; they also refused to recognize that any
authority—including their own elected leadership—was truly
legitimate. Accordingly, they raised an anarchistic "popular
clamor" every time that someone suggested that they should
honor, elevate, follow, or obey wise and virtuous leaders.[5]

The founders went to great lengths to persuade American
men to keep their passions in check and to obey their elected and
appointed political officials. They appealed to American men's
reason and virtue. They called on religious leaders and secular
educators to teach men greater self-discipline and patriotic sentiment. They framed innovative constitutions and engineered
political institutions to neutralize men's passions, reduce their
conflicts, and strengthen the legitimacy of public officials. Importantly, they also called forth the dominant standards of manhood to shame disorderly men into good behavior. The
founders often stigmatized disorderly males by accusing them of
"effeminacy." Let me provide some examples.

Samuel Adams expected mature men to avoid the slavery to
desire and luxury that he thought typical of women. He con-

demned as effeminate any man who engaged in self-indulgent
or spendthrift behavior. Samuel Williams spelled out the long-
term implications of such male effeminacy. He claimed that the
spread of male self-indulgence was likely to produce "an emaci-
ated feeble race, degraded by effeminacy and weakness." The
emerging generation would be "unmanly" and "incapable of
manly exertions." The predictable outcome was that effeminate
youths would lack the self-discipline and civic virtue to fortify
their family fortunes or to defend the nation.[6] Male effeminacy
made America a nation at risk.

Supporters of the American Revolution demanded that
American males measure up to manhood in stark contrast to effeminate British troops. Samuel Adams challenged Boston patriots: "If you are men, behave like men." Moses Mather
implored American rebels "to nobly play the man for our country." Other leaders called on American males to "fight manfully
for their country." How could an ill-equipped, disorganized
American military force defeat Britain's extraordinarily powerful imperial army and navy? Many founders felt that the patriots
had one important advantage. American militiamen were manly
soldiers in comparison to the effeminate British officer corps.
Thus, Mercy Otis Warren criticized British General Howe for
enjoying "effeminate and reprehensible pleasures" while at-
tending a "handsome adulteress" in Philadelphia rather than
planning and executing military strategy against the Continental Army. The American press commonly condemned British officers as effeminate aristocrats who led legions of lazy, ignorant,
and disorderly Red Coats.[7]

After the Revolution, the founders often defined mature
manhood in opposition to the effeminacy of disorderly males.
When federalist newspapers criticized the American farmers
who participated in a 1786 tax protest known as Shays's Rebellion, they first attacked the agrarian rebels for unpatriotic behavior and then accused them of effeminacy. Journalists alleged that
western Massachusetts farmers were steeped in luxury and com-
promised by corruption. They were obsessed with feathers, gau-

zes, and ribbons. They were ruled by their wives. And they deserved to be discredited by their erratic actions, which identified them with disorderly women.[8] The founders connected all marginal men with women. They associated unruly bachelors with the effeminate fop. They attired court-martialed soldiers in women's clothing before marching them out of camp. They also condemned Indian males and male slaves for being effeminate. Marginal males appeared to be effeminate because—like women—they lacked manly independence, family governance, and accepted public presence.

MARGINAL MALES

The founders dwelled on men's lustful tendencies, which were manifested in commonplace vices such as masturbation, premarital sex, and adultery. Men's repeated failure to discipline their sexual desires symbolized a broader and more dangerous trend. The founders were extremely apprehensive that American men regularly failed to restrain the personal passions, impulses, avarice, and aggression that threatened the new nation's moral, economic, social, and political order.

Young men were prone to sexual transgressions. Benjamin Franklin, Thomas Jefferson, and George Washington all admitted their own youthful lust. They regularly warned young men to stay away from low women, seductive women, prostitutes, and, sometimes, all females. Often, their advice fell on deaf ears. In New York City, for example, crowds of young libertines were known to loiter about the streets and make sexually suggestive remarks to the single women who walked by. A number of young men went beyond provocative words to violent deeds. They were subject to rape charges. Founding-era criminologists considered rape to be a crime that was rooted in men's "abuse" of natural passions and their "frenzy" of deep desires. The rapist was like all men—only he was more abusive and more frenzied.[9]

The founders also believed that same-sex relationships constituted dangerous transgressions of decency. They saw male-male

sex as a potential in the lustful nature of all impassioned men. In
Puritan communities sodomy was considered a mortal sin
against God. In secular circles, sodomy was considered an excess
of passion and an abuse of nature. Why were private sexual acts
among consenting adult males a public concern? The main reason was that same-sex relations frustrated the institution of marriage. Men who engaged in sodomy unleashed their passions in
a way that worked against the stable, patriarchal family life that
calmed both female and male passions.

The young males considered most likely to subvert patriarchal family life were "bachelors of age"—men who made it to
their mid-twenties without having settled into marriage, fatherhood, and family responsibility. Many of them ridiculed marriage and family life as invitations to slavery and boredom.
Bachelor lustfulness, selfishness, and irresponsibility were common themes in early American literature. Male protagonists
were forever plotting to destroy girls' chastity and acquire their
family fortunes. Meanwhile, social critics complained that licentious bachelors set bad examples for impressionable boys.
Bachelors bragged about their conquests and deceits only to
tempt youths into misguided notions of manhood. Benjamin
Franklin considered bachelors to be less than mature men. They
were half-men (or women) who needed to be governed.[10]

Many founders felt that young white slave owners also
needed to be governed. These young men engaged in "early, excessive, and enervating indulgences" by having sex with their female slaves. Sometimes, young masters raped slave women who
were their own half-sisters or aunts. They also fathered new
slaves only to degrade, tyrannize, and sell their sons and make
their daughters victims of their own incestuous desires. Many
founders felt that the only creature on earth who was more de-
praved than a debauched young white master was a disorderly
black male slave. White leaders depicted black male slaves as out-
casts from humanity and associated them with uncontrollable
lust, sexual violence, and rebellion. The boisterous passions of

both masters and slaves prompted Thomas Jefferson to express grave fears for the future of the nation.[11]

Young white males known as the "strolling poor" were more often identified with law-breaking than sexual transgression. They were roving youths who went from town to town in search of work, or land, or adventure. Residents generally greeted them with grave distrust. After all, they were young and rootless—threats to men's property as well as to women's virtue. Local officials interrogated and "warned out" strangers. They gave them a few days to secure a sponsor, post a bond, or leave. Those who did not comply were likely to be punished and then escorted out of town. In the larger towns and cities, the ranks of strolling poor were bloated by large numbers of "vagrants" and "paupers"—poor men reputed to wed poverty to immorality. Civic leaders warned that widespread vagrancy and pauperism along with drinking, gambling, prostitution, adultery, fighting, dueling, thievery, and murder constituted a terrifying trend toward male degeneracy in America.[12]

Near cousins to degenerate urban males were white backwoodsmen who lived on the frontier. Most American leaders considered backwoodsmen to be vicious men living in a wilderness where there was little law or authority to regulate their conduct. They were an intemperate, greedy, aggressive bunch prone to thievery and violence. White backwoodsmen met their disruptive match in disorderly Indian males. Although many founders admired Indian cultures, they usually degraded Indian males for being barbaric and effeminate. Some founders even felt that Indians' penchant for alcohol was part of God's divine plan to eliminate these "savages" from the face of the earth.

What should be done with marginal males who threatened to spread lust, moral degeneracy, mob chaos, and frontier violence across the American landscape? The founders never intended "all men" to receive equal liberty. That would have been suicidal. In their minds, equal liberty for libertines, bachelors, slave owners, itinerants, vagrants, paupers, and backwoodsmen would have transformed liberty into license, destroyed social harmony, and subverted political order. Furthermore, equal liberty for nonwhite males was even less conceivable. Most founders felt that these marginal men had to be excluded from citizenship and subjected to discipline in order to ensure at least a semblance of public order.

The founders practiced two forms of exclusionary politics among males. First, they agreed that men deserved equal liberty if they met a series of formal requirements for casting a vote, sitting on a jury, running for office, or serving in the militia. Most American jurisdictions had property, residency, and age requirements that were sufficient to exclude libertines, wanderers, vagrants, paupers, and backwoodsmen from citizenship. Most jurisdictions also had racial and religious requirements that excluded Indian and black males (along with other non-Protestants) from exercising citizenship rights. Second, the founders generally agreed that men deserved equal liberty if they met a series of informal requirements for being admitted to civil society and political participation. Clearly, the single-most important informal requirement was that they voluntarily forsake self-indulgent bachelorhood for stable marriage.

MANHOOD, MARRIAGE, AND STABILITY

The dominant standards of manhood declared that young men should first establish their independence and then, at the earliest appropriate age, settle down into stable marriages to provision, protect, and govern their own families. Parents, teachers, ministers, civic leaders, and writers conspired to convince young men that they ought to acquire a sufficient economic stake to support a family, marry a respectable woman, sire children, and perpetuate their family lines. The founders offered five major reasons why otherwise disorderly young men should mature into manhood by voluntarily assuming the burdens of family responsibility.

First, the founders urged young men to marry to bring love, affection, and a sense of meaning to their lives. A seventeen-year-old Alexander Hamilton held the increasingly widespread, sentimental view that love was "doubly sweet in wedlock's holy bands." Hamilton's sentimentality was reinforced by Judith Sargent Murray's reminder that the bachelor's existence was barren. She wrote, "The life of the bachelor is almost invariably gloomy" if not "truly pitiable." The bachelor had neither a soul-mate to enrich his life nor any sons to carry on his family line.[13] When it came to personal happiness and fulfillment, marriage was the clear choice.

Second, the founders promoted marriage as an opportunity for young men to demonstrate their manhood. Heading a family was a complex challenge. A young man had to give up a bachelor's slavery to passion without exchanging it for a husband's slavery to a wife. Initially, a young husband showed manly self-discipline by giving up the drinking, gambling, promiscuity, itinerancy, and other vices associated with footloose single life. Gradually, he had to exhibit manly merit by achieving family mastery. He fashioned himself into an authoritative family patriarch who governed his wife, children, and other dependents. Ideally, he wielded his patriarchal authority with so much skill and gentleness that his wife did not feel so much burdened as blessed by his caring rule.

Third, the founders proposed marriage as means to transform immature youths into responsible adults. Benjamin Franklin claimed that marriage was "the cause of all good order in the world and what alone preserves it from the utmost confusion."[14] A young married man assumed family responsibilities. He was no longer concerned solely with his own pleasure or fortune. Now he had to work hard to procure the good of his family. He had to be more serious about cultivating his farm, following his trade, or pursuing his business. His maturing effort, attitudes, and work ethic would earn him the respect and trust of other men as well as a manly reputation for being someone who kept his promises, acted with civility, and conformed to the rules of civil society. A married male fit into responsible, adult society.

Fourth, the founders suggested that marriage gave men a stake in the public good. A married man was presumed to be dedicated to his family's welfare. He would sacrifice his own pleasures to protect his children by fulfilling their economic needs and by joining with other men in militia units to take up arms against local criminals and foreign enemies. Ideally, men who learned to make sacrifices for their particular families simultaneously learned to make sacrifices for their larger families, their local community and the nation. They became protectors and patriots who defended liberty and risked their lives for their wives and their children as well as for their fellow countrymen. Family patriarchy was a school for male civic virtue and citizenship.

A fifth crucial reason for marriage was that it exposed young men and women to each other's positive influence. On the one hand, a husband who governed his wife firmly but lovingly was able to monitor her behavior, keep her focused on her domestic duties, and thereby prevent her from causing disorder in family life and public life. Responsible family patriarchs were America's first line of defense against disorderly women. On the other hand, a wise husband allowed himself to be exposed to the civilizing influence of a republican woman. His republican wife would guard him against corruption, reclaim him from vice, and encourage him to become a peaceful, respectable, patriotic citizen. The founders were convinced that the cooperative ideal of republican marriage had the potential to transform both men and women into more reliable, more pliable, more orderly people.

In summary, the founders felt that marriage fostered among men a sufficient sense of contentment, self-discipline, responsibility, stability, and patriotism to ensure that most family men would exercise liberty with restraint, assume the status of sober workers and neighbors, and generally obey legitimate laws. This presumptive trust in married men's good behavior helped to persuade skeptics that average family men also should be trusted with the rights and responsibilities of citizenship. For example, Fisher Ames generally detested democracy. He thought most men were passionate and disorderly, and he wanted to exclude most of them from participating in politics. However, Ames supported voting rights for "citizens who have families and children" because their wives and children functioned as "the pledges of their fidelity."[15] Like Ames, many founders saw the marriage license as the cure for male license.

Of course, a marriage license at best was a partial cure for disorderly male behavior. Many husbands engaged in adultery regardless of their marriage vows. Many family patriarchs proved to be poor providers and irresponsible protectors. Many men deserted their families only to leave their wives penniless and their children fatherless. It was easy to get married but it was a lifelong challenge to behave like a mature family man. Many men never rose to the challenge and others failed to sustain marital fidelity over time.

At the other extreme, some men were so obsessively devoted to their families that they neglected their neighbors and the nation. During the Revolution, husbands often refused to leave their families to serve in the militia. Many married militia soldiers demobilized at the first opportunity and returned to their families even though they were desperately needed on the battlefront. Other married soldiers deserted their units to hasten their return to their homes. All in all, the founders believed that married men were far more orderly than bachelors but they also recognized that husbands retained bachelor-like tendencies manifested in disorderly if not criminal behavior.

CONFRONTING CRIME

The founders were quite concerned about males who engaged in crime. What they perceived as widespread tendencies toward criminality among men threatened public order in two ways. First, men who robbed, raped, and murdered created the basis for ongoing conflicts with their victims and their victims' families and friends. Second, lawbreaking was infectious. If some men broke the law with "impunity" (no fear of punishment), other impassioned, impulsive, and avaricious men would surely follow their example. The founders had to confront crime to ensure order in the republic.

During the colonial era, American officials subjected criminals to two primary penalties: capital punishment and public humiliation. Capital punishment was attached to a great many crimes, but it was rarely carried out. The main sanction for convicted men was some form of public humiliation. Most male criminals were sentenced to public whippings, brandings, the pillory, or degrading public labor. Officials' main goal was not so much to inflict pain on the guilty as to make perpetrators feel so ashamed and humiliated that they would commit no more crimes. Simultaneously, townspeople who observed criminals' public humiliation would be deterred from engaging in any future lawbreaking.

After the Revolution, reformers questioned the legitimacy of capital punishment and public humiliation. These practices seemed to contradict revolutionary norms of rationality and benevolence. Perhaps more important, they apparently failed to deter crime. Critics contended, for example, that the spectacle of a public hanging actually invited more crime by providing degenerate male criminals with an unearned opportunity to redeem their lost manhood and their reputations. In 1788 "A Citizen of the World" complained that audiences at hangings were more concerned with the conduct of the condemned than with the justice of the sentence: "The populace depart, either applauding the criminal's hardness, or as they term it, his spirit, in 'dying like a cock'—or else condemning his weakness—'He died like a d——d chicken hearted dog.' " To die like a cock was to be remembered as a man, as if a manly performance on the scaffold erased a lifetime of heinous crimes.[16]

Reformers also argued that punishments involving public humiliation were counterproductive. On the one hand, criminals' mere presence in public places was dangerous. The penal scene where convicts performed public labor drew spectators who might be influenced by the felons. One Philadelphia official opposed public punishments such as street cleaning and road repairs because they gave convicts an opportunity to engage innocent boys in indecent conversation. Criminality was infectious and epidemic. It needed to be quarantined. On the other hand, the mere sight of convicts being whipped or weighed down by a ball and chain often elicited public sympathy. Sometimes spectators showered admiration on convicts who exemplified manly fortitude. They showed compassion for men suffering obvious distress. And they expressed disdain toward penal officials who inflicted the distress.

Reformers' main alternative to public punishment was imprisonment in an innovative institution called a penitentiary, or "house of repentance." The idea of jailing convicts for prolonged periods was based on a belief that prisoners could experience penitence, undertake rehabilitation, and redeem their manhood by regaining their independence and family status. An imprisoned male lost his independence and family and thereby suffered emasculation. Benjamin Rush wanted to push emasculation as far as possible. He suggested that convicts be sent to isolated penitentiaries: "Let a large house . . . be erected in a remote part of the state. Let the avenue to this house be rendered difficult and gloomy by mountains or morasses. Let its doors be of iron; and let the grating, occasioned by opening and shutting them, be increased by an echo from a neighboring mountain, that shall extend and continue a sound that shall deeply pierce the soul." Within soul-piercing penitentiaries, the older convicts would be isolated from the younger ones and the most vicious criminals would be locked into isolation cells. Inmate Samuel Quarrier bewailed the consequences: "This ignominious imprisonment unmans the heart."[17]

The notion that imprisonment "unmans" the heart was another way of saying that prison officials treated convicts like dependent women or children. However, penitentiary officials also wanted to provide convicts an opportunity to regain their lost manhood. They encouraged prisoners to search their souls, rethink right and wrong, experience regret and penitence for their crimes, reorder their priorities, control their passions, and learn useful trades in preparation for their return to society. Ideally, all convicts could be rehabilitated. Then they would be freed from the penitentiary and returned to the honorable status of independent men, family patriarchs, and productive citizens.

The potential for prisoner rehabilitation was tied to the belief that penitentiaries could motivate men to discipline desire, especially sexual desire. In the 1780s, Philadelphia leaders complained of "a general intercourse between the criminals of the different sexes" resulting in "scenes of debauchery." They also thought that an "inadequate provision of bedding" was conducive to same-sex contact among male inmates. When the old Walnut Street jail was converted into a penitentiary, officials separated male and female convicts to prevent sexual contact. They also sought to improve prison sleeping conditions as a means to eliminate sodomy. In such a controlled environment, reformers felt confident that criminals would learn to discipline desire and become mature men.[18]

By 1805, Philadelphia's experiment with penitentiaries spread to New York, New Jersey, Connecticut, Massachusetts, and Virginia. What made penitentiaries innovative was that they employed state coercion not simply to control and discipline male criminals but to transform them into responsible adults and good citizens. Like marriage, penitentiaries promised to liberate disorderly males from their slavery to desire and put them on the path of reason. Like republican wives, penitentiaries were supposed to transform disorderly males into independent persons, responsible family men, and law-abiding citizens. When penitentiaries worked the way they were meant to work, "the offender becomes humbled and reformed, [and] society, instead of losing, gains a citizen."[19]

It is important to point out that the founders' faith in male rehabilitation was qualified in two ways. First, it focused exclusively on white males. The founders saw black males as lower-order creatures ("cattle") who lacked the manly ability to discipline their passions. Indeed, black male slaves could not even be proper family patriarchs because slave status prevented them from protecting, provisioning, or governing their women and children. If blacks could not be "men," then they could not be rehabilitated to manhood. Similarly, most founders felt that Indian males could never measure up to manhood or be rehabilitated to it. Whites did not consider Indian males sufficiently independent or patriarchal to qualify for manhood. Many founders felt that Indian males were uncivilized and, worse yet, subordinated to wives who grew the crops and participated in tribal politics. If Indian husbands were inherently effeminate, then they too could not be reformed.

Second, the founders' faith in male reform was limited by their still-modest expectations regarding most men. Family men as well as those criminals who regained their freedom, resumed their status as family heads, and now voted in elections, could be trusted and empowered *only so far*. They still shared the darker side of men's nature. They were passionate, impulsive, avaricious creatures subject to mob enthusiasms and criminal relapses. Furthermore, average family patriarchs and rehabilitated criminals lacked the experience, wisdom, and virtue needed to guide and administer a new nation fragmented by internal conflict and surrounded by powerful enemies. Most founders were willing to grant limited citizenship to males who measured up to the dominant standards of manhood but they were convinced that a small elite group of men was needed to govern the nation.

CONCLUSION

The American founders believed that "all men" had an abstract capacity to be free and equal but they feared that most men indulged passion, impulse, interest, and aggression only to cause disorder in public life. Their primary outlook on manhood and politics can be summarized as follows:

1. A mature man was an independent male who disciplined his passions, assumed family responsibilities, governed women and dependents, fit into society, and contributed to civic life. A mature man was a "not-woman."

2. Most men did not measure up to manhood. They acted on passion, impulse, and avarice, and used liberty as an excuse for engaging in disorderly conduct. The founders consider such men to be unmanly, or "effeminate."

3. The founders stigmatized libertines, bachelors, itinerants, vagrants, paupers, slave owners, slaves, backwoodsmen, and Indians and excluded most of them from public life.

4. The founders' main cure for disorderly white men was marriage to republican women and, for white criminals, penitence and rehabilitation to manhood, freedom, and family.

Men who were slaves to passion could not be trusted with basic citizenship. They had to be excluded from politics, reformed through marriage, or rehabilitated in a penitentiary.

Many founders felt that male maturity was a necessary qualification for citizenship but it was not a sufficient qualification for leadership. Perhaps the average family man was qualified to produce crops and pay taxes, obey laws, vote for representatives, sit on juries, or serve in the militia. However, most founders doubted that the average family man was qualified to deliberate on the major public issues of the day, instruct representatives who were wiser and more virtuous, take part in decision making, negotiate trade agreements and treaties, resolve crises, or recognize and realize historical opportunities. What America needed was not more citizen participation but more guidance and governance by a few exceptional men.

CHAPTER 5

A Small Governing Elite

Noah Webster feared that America's male majority suffered from "rough passions." That was why he could not even trust relatively responsible, stable family men to get deeply involved in politics and govern the nation. Ordinary men lacked the self-discipline, virtue, experience, and talent needed to guide America through political protests, revolution, re-constitution of governments, internal dissension, and threats of foreign intervention. Ordinary men also lacked the historical insight and intellectual foresight needed to lead America into an uncertain but promising future. Webster was convinced that men's disorders and democracy's excesses had to be tempered by a national government that was administered by a select few men. Indeed, many founders ranked democratic ideals secondary to what they considered the necessary leadership and authority of a small governing elite.

NATURAL ARISTOCRATS

John Adams observed that men were born with a "passion for distinction." They not only wanted to be accepted by other men; they also wanted to rise above other men, stand out from other men, and achieve a degree of celebrity among men. Adams

applauded this passion for distinction because it encouraged
men to do the unselfish patriotic deeds that might win them
public recognition and reward. He knew, however, that the passion for distinction had a dark side. It could foster jealousy, envy,
and violence among some men. Mercy Otis Warren also observed both aspects of men's ambitions. She agreed that men's
passion for distinction was "a noble principle" but she worried
that it could produce among men "mortifying instances of profligacy, tyranny, and the wanton exercise of arbitrary sway." Most
founding fathers and founding mothers praised men's desire for
celebrity as an important source of their "manly and martial
spirit" but they also worried that men's ambition for "pomp,
power, and greatness" would corrupt them.[1]

The highest object of men's passion for distinction was fame
among the living and remembrance by future generations. The
most appropriate and honorable means to achieve fame and remembrance was for individuals to perform great deeds of military courage and political leadership that would earn them
widespread public recognition and especially the praise of worthy men. Ideally, a few individuals would accomplish such heroic
deeds and achieve so much celebrity that, immediately, they
would be honored by all of their contemporaries and then, after
death, they would be lovingly remembered by family descendants and future citizens. The founders' consensus was that men
in search of fame sought to perform heroic deeds and render
themselves immortal.

George Washington exemplified the quest for fame, its
achievement, and its payoff. He admitted that he was driven by a
nearly obsessive desire for fame. He wanted his military service
and his public service to be recognized and rewarded not with
money (which he regularly refused) but with eternal fame
(which he craved). And he was remarkably successful. Washington became a legend in his own lifetime. Patriots took it upon
themselves to pronounce and perpetuate his fame and immor-
tality. For example, the Reverend George Duffield called on
Americans to "let the illustrious Washington . . . live perpetual in

the minds and the praises of all." He told his audience to "aid feeble fame with her hundred wings and tongues to proclaim his worth; and . . . convey down through every age the unsullied remembrance of the patriot, the hero, and citizen combined, and deliver his name and his praise to the unbounded ocean of immortal esteem." Americans adored Washington as "a man among men," memorialized him as a national hero, and still honor him two hundred years later.[2]

The manly rhetoric of fame had an important political effect. It made powerful leadership seem relatively safe. Only a select few men merited great acclaim and fewer still achieved great fame. The founders portrayed these accomplished and adored men as natural leaders. Their heroic deeds demonstrated their special merit. Their fame testified to their ability to attract the admiration and support of other men. Many founders felt that these rare and remarkable individuals were such outstanding men and exceptional leaders of men that Americans' deep-seated fears of powerful public officials inviting political tyranny simply did not apply to them. America's famous men could be trusted to wield great power without significant checks and balances.

Consider the views of Thomas Jefferson. Jefferson regularly warned his countrymen against putting great power into the hands of political leaders. While in France, he read a copy of the proposed U.S. Constitution. His main criticism was that it placed no limits on a president's tenure in office. The same man could be reelected every four years and become a virtual monarch for life who was likely to abuse his authority and destroy men's liberties. Nevertheless, Jefferson was willing to suspend his fears of abusive presidential power when George Washington was inaugurated as the first president. Jefferson came out against presidential term limits "during the life of our great leader" because he considered Washington's "executive talents" superior to those of all other men. Jefferson was convinced that Washington alone, "by the authority of his name and the confidence reposed in his perfect integrity, is fully qualified to put the new government under way so as to secure it against the efforts of opposition."[3] Most founders felt that Washington was such an exceptional man and leader that he should be empowered and trusted, not restrained and resisted.

Furthermore, most founders were confident that the ordinary family man and citizen would empower exceptional leaders and trust them to do the right thing. The average family man sought his small share of fame by siring sons to honor him, remember him, and continue his family name and family line for the indefinite future. Accordingly, the average husband and father was predisposed to respect a great leader who sought to be remembered and memorialized by future generations. In a Fourth of July speech, Simeon Baldwin employed the rhetoric of fame to foster a bond of shared manhood between family men and political leaders. Baldwin praised common men who worked for "the protection of their estates, families, persons, fame, and lives" and he applauded great political leaders who sought to transmit "their names, their virtues, and their noble deeds to posterity, by whom they will be revered as the most distinguished benefactors of mankind and eminent examples for future generations."[4] The rhetoric of fame encouraged family men to identify with great leaders as well as to honor and obey them.

Most founders agreed that extraordinary leaders needed to be honored and obeyed. They were crucial national assets. Their great virtues, talents, and achievements elevated them above the common herd and earned them widespread recognition and great public confidence. They constituted a select elite that was greatly needed to guide and govern the nation while simultaneously winning the consent and compliance of citizens. The founders called this elite "the natural aristocracy." It was made up of great men who *merited* their high status and political authority by promoting the public good and earning public support. It was quite different from Europe's artificial aristocracy which was made up of upper-class men who *inherited* their high status and political authority by being born into titled families.

Virtually all founders agreed on the existence of a natural aristocracy, but many disagreed about its integrity and its likely reception among citizens. Federalists (founders who supported the U.S. Constitution) often spoke in favor of the natural aristocracy. Alexander Hamilton argued that the Constitution invited natural aristocrats to lead the nation. Their good deeds inspired public trust. Robert R. Livingston praised the natural aristocracy as a repository of men's virtue, wisdom, eminence, and learning. He asked, "Does a man possess the confidence of his fellow citizens for having done them important services? He is an aristocrat. Has he great integrity? Such a man will be greatly trusted. He is an aristocrat."[5] Most federalists believed that only a small elite demonstrated the great merit needed to be ranked among the natural aristocracy; and only this small elite was qualified to guide and govern the nation.

Anti-federalists (founders who opposed the U.S. Constitution) agreed that a natural aristocracy existed within the ranks of men. New Yorker Melancton Smith affirmed that "the author of nature has bestowed on some greater capacities than on others—birth, education, talents, and wealth, creating distinctions among men as visible and of as much influence as titles, stars, and garters." These men constituted a "natural aristocracy," and they were likely to "command influence and respect among the common people." Anti-federalists' main criticism was that natural aristocrats were just as vulnerable to corruption as other men and, perhaps, even more so. Many of them harbored a deep "love of domination." Alas, even national heroes with "the greatest purity of intention," if given the opportunity, were likely to become tyrants.[6]

One factor that tempered the debate over the trustworthiness versus the corruptibility of the natural aristocracy was a broad American consensus that two unique men, Benjamin Franklin and George Washington, deserved special honors for their exceptional manhood and political heroics. Federalists referred to them as "distinguished worthies" and called on citizens to show their respect by supporting the U.S. Constitution that

Franklin and Washington helped draft. Anti-federalists rarely attacked Franklin and Washington. At times, they even congratulated citizens for their propensity to honor these national heroes. Anti-federalists' main opposition tactic was to point out that each citizen was responsible for making his own independent judgment about the Constitution. A good citizen certainly should love Franklin and Washington but he was still dutybound to evaluate the Constitution and make his own thoughtful decision about whether to support or oppose ratification.[7]

In summary, most founders were convinced that men had a passion for distinction manifested in a quest for fame that elevated a few select men into a natural aristocracy of political leaders. Although most founders recognized the existence of a natural aristocracy, some Americans opposed its special claims to leadership and a great many Americans proved to be uncomfortable with the *language* of natural aristocracy. John Adams learned this lesson the hard way. He regularly spoke about natural aristocrats only to find himself constantly on the defensive. He repeatedly distinguished America's natural aristocrats from Europe's hereditary nobility but his critics insisted that Adams's principles meant "hereditary power and hereditary privileges." Thomas Jefferson was more politically astute. He fully agreed that the natural aristocracy was a "most precious gift of nature" but he also knew that all talk about aristocracy was repugnant to American citizens.[8] Following Jefferson's example, many founders chose to avoid using aristocratic terminology and instead discussed political leadership in patriarchal language.

THE PATRIARCHAL LANGUAGE
OF LEADERSHIP

The founders had a mixed view of elite leadership. They led a revolution against a powerful king. They drafted state constitutions that limited executive discretion. They framed a U.S. Constitution that fragmented national political authority. Most founders agreed with Jefferson that men's liberties were imperiled whenever leaders had sufficient power and opportunity to crush them. Nevertheless, most founders continued to believe that the struggling new nation needed powerful, decisive leadership to survive early threats of disorder and to thrive in difficult times. Their discussions about the need for strong political leadership often employed patriarchal language. They portrayed great leaders as national fathers and political father figures.

The American founders inherited their ideals of political leadership from Great Britain. One of the most influential British tracts on political leadership was Lord Bolingbroke's *The Idea of a Patriot King*. Bolingbroke promoted the image of a Patriot King as a majestic leader. He governed like a "common father" and treated the people as part of his "patriarchal family." A Patriot King had a "love of liberty," and he defended and extended liberty to his national family. He displayed affection for citizens and exhibited clemency by reforming rather than exacting retribution from any "rebellious children." A Patriot King also epitomized manhood. He acted with integrity and civility, refused the lures of flattery, resisted factionalism, practiced manly virtues, and avoided unmanly vices. His virtues and accomplishments earned him pervasive public gratitude, which enabled him to rule on the basis of widespread consent. Ideally, a Patriot King was "reverenced and obeyed" in life and accorded "fame after death."[9]

Although the founders opposed the idea of kingship and the rule of kings, they regularly employed Bolingbroke's patriarchal language to affirm the need for strong political leadership for America. In the 1770s for example, Gad Hitchcock addressed public officials as "honored fathers" and "civic fathers," and Phillips Payson called them "civil fathers." In the 1780s Samuel Cooper described the framers of the Articles of Confederation as "fathers of their country" filled with "parental tenderness"; Samuel McClintock honored New Hampshire's framers as "fathers and guardians of their people"; and Samuel Langdon spoke of America's public leaders as "fathers of a large family." In the 1790s Israel Evans told the country's political "fathers" that citi-

zens would "be their political children as long as they are good
parents"; Timothy Stone instructed officials to be "civil fathers"
and treat citizens with the "tender care of natural parents"; Judith Sargent Murray asserted that men wanted a guardian power
and gave him "the august title—The Father of his Country";
and Peres Fobes noted that "a ruler is the father of his country."[10] Such expressions of patriarchal political leadership were
commonplace for many, many decades after the Revolution.

The founders often used this patriarchal language to make
strong leaders seem more fatherly and caring, less dangerous
and despotic. Presumably a powerful public leader wrapped in
the mantle of benign fatherhood would appear to most citizens
as a dedicated statesman who could be trusted to act for the
good of his political family. That was why federalist James Wilson declared that, under the proposed U.S. Constitution, the
new president would not be a tyrant but a beloved father figure
who would "watch over the whole with paternal care and affection." Federalists felt particularly fortunate that America's
greatest father figure, George Washington, became the first
president. Ministers, writers, and citizens as well as political allies portrayed Washington as "the father of the country," or
"our political father," or "the great father of his country." When
Washington died, he was eulogized as "the father, friend, bene-
factor, and bulwark of his country."[11] Most Americans perceived
him as a national father figure whose manly integrity and civic
achievements animated citizen confidence in his leadership and
neutralized popular fears of potential tyranny.

Equally important, the founders' use of patriarchal language
encouraged American men to obey strong political leaders without feeling that they had to sacrifice their own manly independence. Most American men were accustomed to patriarchal
authority. They were told to obey and honor their own fathers
and they expected their sons to obey and honor them. Understanding this, political leaders regularly presented themselves as
"civic fathers" in the hope and expectation that citizens would
treat them with the same deference and respect that they gener-

ally bestowed on their own family fathers or grandfathers. Simultaneously, the founders' use of patriarchal language made political dissent more daunting. It was one thing to struggle against a tyrannical king but quite another to rebel against a caring father figure.

Most founders accepted, applauded, and even celebrated this conjuncture of fatherhood and politics. They venerated America's ancestral fathers for pioneering the continent. They honored America's colonial fathers for their courageous defense of liberty against British tyranny. They memorialized America's revolutionary fathers for beating the odds to achieve independence. And they continued to congratulate America's civic fathers for founding new states and a glorious new nation. Sometimes, the founders' praise for political father figures served as a prelude to expressing their underlying fear that the age of great patriarchal leaders was over. "Where are our fathers?" cried Stanley Griswold in 1801. "Where are our former men of dignity . . . who in their day appeared like men?" Alas, American males seemed to be "more disposed to act like children than men."[12] Could the nation survive without reproducing new generations of great political father figures?

Many speakers, writers, and politicians believed that America needed great patriarchal leaders and beloved father figures "to guide with a steady hand in tempestuous seasons." America would not survive its infancy without the leadership of heroic men who had the ability "to lead and advise [the public] in the more boisterous and alarming as well as in calm and temperate seasons."[13] Who were these exceptional men? Why were they so desperately needed?

THE CODE OF POLITICAL MANHOOD

Being national father figure could be a challenging task. A great political leader sometimes had to forgo popularity and ignore legality, for example, when confronting the domestic crises that called forth the Constitutional Convention in 1787, or when addressing the foreign policy dilemmas that prompted

President Washington to issue a Proclamation of Neutrality in 1793, or when taking advantage of the historic opportunities afforded by President Jefferson's purchase of the Louisiana Territory in 1803. Most founders believed that a great political leader had to scale the heights of manhood and rise above the ordinary rules of public life to meet the urgent needs of a promising new nation.

The founders subscribed to an informal but influential code of political manhood that required worthy leaders to refuse to solicit or even enjoy a crude popularity among disorderly men who, after all, were more disposed to the self-indulgent deceptions of vanity and flattery than to the manly integrity of virtue and reason. Seeking the approval of degraded, dependent men was always foolish. It was also effeminate. Political leaders who sought or settled for a crude popularity demonstrated their lack of manly independence. They enslaved themselves to the whims and fancies of the most fickle and superficial public opinion. In contrast, a manly political leader kept to "the plain path of duty." He always did what he considered right, reasonable, and conscionable. His integrity usually won him the respect as well as the consent and compliance of the most sober and mature citizens.

Great political leaders understood that they often paid a short-term political price for exhibiting manly integrity. By remaining unmoved by boisterous opposition, undaunted by popular protests, and undismayed by threats of imminent danger, they were likely to suffer the envy, anger, spite, and mischief of lesser men. America's first three presidents—George Washington, John Adams, and Thomas Jefferson—complained often that they had to fortify and defend themselves against the unwarranted "calumny" of callous critics, irrational mobs, and dangerous demagogues. Great political leaders were almost certain to encountered the periodic wrath of significant portions of the impassioned male majority.

A leader's manhood and political worth were tested by his response to periodic public wrath. A manly leader kept in mind that he was forever obligated to support "a manly opposition . . .

to popular prejudice and vulgar error." Sometimes, he was obliged to expose a "favorite error" of the public to "avert national ruin" only to excite the public's resentment. His willingness to serve the public good and withstand the public's resentment was important evidence of his statesmanship. Furthermore, a great political leader saw the conflict between political manhood and popularity as a challenge. The challenge for Patrick Henry was to exhibit "manly fortitude" and "manly firmness" against "an erring world." Others talked about pitting manly "integrity" and "intrepidity" against "public execration." Ultimately, a great political leader demonstrated that he was man enough to bear the weight of great public antagonism. A lesser man collapsed under it and was thereby reduced to "a crouching and fawning disposition [that] takes the place of manliness."[14]

The founders' code of political manhood also required that a great leader exercise the highest form of manly independence: *political prerogative.* The founders identified personal independence and economic independence as crucial male virtues because they enabled a man to think and act solely on the basis of his own conscience, reason, and will. A manly political leader took independence one decisive step further. He declared himself free to think and act not only for himself but also for the public good solely on the basis of his own conscience, reason, and will. Put differently, he claimed the political prerogative to do whatever he thought necessary for the public good regardless of adverse public opinion, significant political opposition, or even legitimate legal obstacles.

Many founders felt that Americans should treasure great and powerful leaders' presence and assist them by insulating them from the complaints and demands of ordinary citizens. Notable founders such as John Adams and Fisher Ames detested the popular clamor for more democracy. They thought it the height of idiocy to believe that ordinary family men should exercise the authority to deliberate on complex public issues, make binding decisions about them, or give mandatory instructions to their elected officials who, in turn, would carry the message of citizen preferences to higher legislative forums. Adams, Ames, and other founders were convinced that only the most impassioned and ignorant Americans would elevate ordinary men to the status of decision makers and thereby demote talented political leaders to the role of messengers. In their view, these ultra-democratic demands only invited the unruly male masses to project their disorderly desires into the national political arena and thereby deprived the nation of the guidance and governance of exceptionally virtuous and talented leaders. Noah Webster argued that allowing citizens to issue mandatory instructions to public officials "unmanned" great leaders by denying them the opportunity to act thoughtfully and independently.[15]

The founders believed that an independent man and a manly political leader refused to subordinate himself to ordinary men. He was not their servant, slave, or child. He was no woman! Rather, he was a mature man with his own conscience, reason, and will. George Washington went so far as to assert that any political leader who ignored his own conscientious convictions and instead followed public instructions was more slave than man. He exclaimed, "What figure . . . must a delegate make who comes [to an assembly] with his hands tied and his judgment forestalled?" Patriot-poet Joel Barlow agreed. He urged officials to ignore adverse public instructions: "When the delegate receives instructions which prove to be contrary to the opinion which he afterwards forms, he ought to presume that his constituents . . . are not well informed on the subject and his duty is to vote according to his conscience." Roger Sherman agreed. He asserted that a political leader was "bound by every principle of justice" to elevate his own conscience over constituent instructions.[16] Founder after founder subscribed to a code of political manhood that urged national leaders to claim the political prerogative to act on the basis of their own convictions and reject errant public opinion for the public's own good.

How far could a manly political leader go in opposing public opinion or public instructions before significant numbers of citizens questioned his legitimacy, refused to comply with his decisions, and got rid of him at the earliest opportunity to do so? Many founders felt that an astute political leader was revered by men less for his brilliant reasoning or profound decision making or astute public policies than for his notable display of exceptional manhood. A great political leader epitomized the dominant norm of independent manhood when he exhibited great self-discipline, courage, fortitude, candor, integrity, and decisiveness by exercising political prerogative amidst public scrutiny, adversity, opposition, and conflict. The founders believed that most men recognized and honored these noble displays of manly independence by granting their consent and compliance—even when they disagreed with leaders' actual decisions. Ultimately, it was great leaders' display of manly character, even more than their policy preferences or political performances, that attracted most men's admiration and support.

That was Jeremiah Wadsworth's viewpoint. He reported several instances when political leaders "disregarded their instructions and have been re-elected." He also cited instances when leaders chained themselves to public opinion only to be "despised" for their unmanly behavior. Alexander Hamilton went further. He suggested that a great leader who withstood citizens' "temporary delusions" in favor of his own "more cool and sedate reflection" not only could save the people "from the fatal consequences of their own mistakes"; he also could procure "lasting monuments of [public] gratitude" when men eventually came to their senses, recognized his political courage, and appreciated his manly, independent action on their behalf. Ironically, great leaders enhanced their long-term power and popularity by selectively saying "no" to the citizenry.[17]

Many founders were far more interested in safeguarding great leaders' political prerogative to pursue the common good than in instituting precautionary measures (such as checks and balances) to prevent leaders from abusing their powers. These founders were confident that a small governing elite that measured up to the highest standards of political manhood could and should be trusted to make crucial public decisions with or without the public's immediate support. These founders argued that Americans should seek out what they considered the better sort of men and then provide them with significant authority to serve the public. That was why relatively radical democratic demands that leaders be rotated out of office after one year's service seemed so absurd to John Adams. He opposed mandatory rotation schemes that limited elected officials to one short term. He believed that these schemes cast out the nation's ablest men and reduced the ranks of leadership to lesser men. Many founders made the point that great leaders were assets. A wise nation treasured their presence rather than squandered their talents.

The founders understood, however, that national leaders who claimed the political prerogative to do whatever they thought necessary regardless of adverse public opinion, political opposition, or legal obstacles were subject to accusations of ruling without the consent of the governed. That was tyranny. How did the founders intend to insulate great leaders against charges of tyranny? Usually, they tried to distinguish a leader's legitimate use of political prerogative from tyrannical rule in two ways. First, they argued that great leaders exercised political prerogative *for the public good* whereas tyrants abused prerogative by using it in the service of their own personal good. Thus, Edmund Randolph claimed that the men who framed the U.S. Constitution were dedicated leaders who assumed the prerogative to reinvent national government because the salvation of the republic was at stake. By contrast, a tyrant exercised political prerogative to enhance his own power, pad his pocket, or satisfy his selfish desires.

Second, the founders' collective memory was filled with the heroic deeds of ancestral fathers and revolutionary leaders who rebelled against established laws and governments to claim extensive authority to make extraordinary history. The founders portrayed these national heroes as daring but caring father figures. By contrast, they depicted the British king as a neglectful, abusive parent who exploited his American offspring. The contrast was visible in American patriots' polar portraits of the two Georges. Patriots depicted George Washington as a national father figure who rightfully asserted political prerogative to establish independence and republican government; but they pictured King George III as a deceitful despot who wrongfully wielded political prerogative only to destroy American men's natural rights and contractual rights as well as to ignore their legitimate protests.

Why did the founders think that Americans so desperately needed a small governing elite of manly leaders to exercise political prerogative for the public good—even if it incurred the public's temporary displeasure and disapprobation? One reason was that the founders were ambivalent about democracy. They extended the reach of liberty and equality beyond British precedents and insisted on securing the consent of most of the (white male) governed—at least in the long run. But they also resisted democratic reforms (such as mandatory public instructions and rotation schemes) that promoted popular self-government and they perpetuated the legitimacy of a small leadership elite. Most founders felt that some democracy was tolerable but too much democracy fostered public disorders that needed to be opposed by strong and wise leaders.

Another reason the founders supported a small governing elite was that they believed the challenges of their times would fix the fate of the nation and the course of the world for many, many years to come. They located themselves at a great historical turning point and, in their minds, the stakes were too high to rely on anyone other than America's most experienced and exceptional men to resolve the terrible crises and realize the marvelous opportunities that would shape the future of Americans and, indeed, all humankind.

A HISTORICAL TURNING POINT

The founders commonly used words such as crisis, contingency, emergency, exigency, and necessity to describe late eighteenth-century American politics. They thought they were living in a historical moment when Enlightenment hopes for achieving human liberty, prosperity, civic virtue, and republican government would be finally realized—or those hopes would be forever destroyed. Most founders were convinced that America needed a few exceptional men to step forward, assume the mantle of leadership, and preside over the course of public affairs to resolve the nation's continuing crises and realize its remarkable opportunities. For them, identifying and empowering manly leaders who would serve as a small governing elite for the nation was an urgent political priority.

During the Revolution, George Washington promoted powerful leadership. He repeatedly argued that both military leaders and civilian officials had a public duty to exercise "extensive powers" in times of crisis and especially in times of war. Although James Madison worried more than Washington about wartime leaders who exercised nearly "dictatorial power" that could easily be abused, Madison did not oppose granting great emergency powers to wartime leaders. Instead, he expressed his sincere hope that the positive outcomes resulting from powerful wartime leadership would more than compensate for the risk of setting a bad precedent and imperiling men's liberties for the future.[18] Nearly all founders agreed that strong, decisive leadership was needed during the times that tried men's souls.

How would the American public react to leaders with nearly dictatorial power? Generally, the founders were convinced that the exercise of strong leadership during crises would receive (and usually did receive) widespread public support. A major crisis aroused public anxiety and motivated citizens to seek strong leaders to resolve the crisis and thereby reduce men's anxiety. In turn, the men's search for strong and effective leaders invited individuals who were ambitious for fame to prove their manly virtue and leadership abilities by exhibiting the self-sacrifice and civic heroism needed to build manly reputations, establish themselves as revered political father figures, and make memorable history.

The Latin root of the word "virtue" is *vir*, which connotes "manliness or prowess." A man who aspired to leadership and fame needed to prove his manly prowess. He had to take "events into his own hands" and shape events "according to his own will." Usually, he was expected to leave women behind in order to perform his patriotic duty and do great deeds among men. For instance, Alexander Hamilton displayed manly prowess when he refused to make "an unmanly surrender" to love. He left his new bride at home so that he could follow the path of public service and accompany General Washington and his army across the continent.[19] Most founders agreed with the ancient belief that heroic men separated themselves from their women to achieve greatness and fame.

Sometimes, a heroic leader had to separate himself from the law as well. Thomas Jefferson certainly supported the rule of law. However, he also recognized that national crises and historical opportunities occasionally demanded that a manly leader undertake extralegal actions. He wrote, "A strict observance of the laws is doubtless one of the high duties . . . but it is not the highest." A great leader had to ignore law and risk infamy "on great occasions when the safety of the nation or some of its very highest interests are at stake." President Jefferson heeded his own words. He ignored law and risked infamy to acquire the Louisiana Territory. He knew that purchasing this vast tract of land required him to act "beyond the Constitution." He considered going through the process of amending the Constitution to gain legal authorization for the purchase, but he decided that the process was too lengthy and uncertain. Ultimately, Jefferson decided to act on his own authority, he claimed, out of a sense of paternal duty. It was "the case of a guardian investing the money of his ward in purchasing an important adjacent territory and saying to him when of age, I did this for your good."[20] Jefferson was convinced that his extralegal act would promote the public good and eventually win most citizens' gratitude and consent.

The periodic elevation of great leaders above legitimate laws during decisive historical moments promised multiple payoffs.

First, a great leader modeled independent manhood. His exhibition of manly prowess, independence, dedication, courage, and prerogative heightened the average man's awareness of his own masculine shortcomings and encouraged him to strive harder to measure up to the dominant standards of mature manhood. Furthermore, a great leader's public presence as a self-disciplined man who transcended personal prejudice, parochial loyalties, and factional politics helped to foster a sense of fraternal solidarity and national pride that brought men closer together. Male bonding helped to maintain public order.

Second, the founders' faith in great leaders who wielded extralegal powers during crises reinforced political patriarchy. By exhibiting such an extreme version of manly independence, great leaders strengthened the essential masculinity of politics and thereby reinforced women's exclusion from public life and subordination to male power. Equally important, national leaders could and did use women's exclusion and subordination as a weapon against their opponents. For example, President George Washington claimed that he made "manly" overtures to strengthen America's position in the world by issuing an extralegal Proclamation of Neutrality as well as by pursuing treaty options with former enemy Great Britain at the expense of former ally France. Alexander Hamilton not only praised Washington for his manly acts; he also denounced critics such as Jefferson and Madison for harboring a "womanish attachment to France." Great leaders exercised manly authority and stigmatized opponents for their effeminacy.[21]

Finally, most founders were convinced that a small governing elite exercising political prerogative could create a great new nation to be enjoyed by all posterity. The men who framed the U.S. Constitution portrayed themselves as exceptional leaders who resolved a national crisis by bringing forth a new republic. They did not dwell on mundane matters of due process and law because, as Edmund Randolph remarked, "There are certainly seasons of a peculiar nature where ordinary cautions must be dispensed with, and this is certainly one of them."[22] James

Madison and Alexander Hamilton agreed that creating a new nation was so important that leaders were free to ignore mundane matters.

The delegates to the Constitutional Convention were originally instructed by Congress to propose revisions to the Articles of Confederation. Shortly after they convened, however, they decided to disregard their instructions and instead put together a plan to reconstitute the national government. Madison felt that a national crisis forced delegates to disregard their instructions and propose a new body politic. "If they had exceeded their powers," he wrote, "they were not only warranted but required by the circumstances in which they were placed to exercise the liberty which they assumed." Madison added, "if they had violated both their powers and obligations in proposing a Constitution," their decision was justified because it was "calculated to accomplish the views and happiness of the people of America."[23]

Madison did not intend to suggest that all extralegal leadership initiatives aimed at resolving national crises and promoting public happiness were legitimate. Rather, he indicated that these extralegal initiatives were warranted when exceptional leaders confronted "the absolute necessity" of defending men's liberty by making "great changes of established governments." In effect, Madison was willing to give great leaders a license to suspend the ordinary rules of public life to defend liberty by creating a new government. In 1776 he argued that America had been blessed with great leaders who instituted momentous changes "by some informal and unauthorized propositions," with "no ill-timed scruples, no zeal for adhering to ordinary forms." Again in 1787, he felt America was blessed with great men who wisely reconfigured the national government.[24]

Hamilton agreed—and then he went further. Hamilton argued that great leaders could suspend ordinary rules and laws not only to found a new nation but also to ensure the safety, prosperity, and influence of an existing nation. He wanted to ensure that national political leaders had sufficient power to address future emergencies and take advantage of future opportunities. He searched the U.S. Constitution's words (for example, "necessary and proper") and concepts (for example, "implied powers") to support an interpretation of the Constitution that provided national political leaders with broad powers to address "necessities of society," which took precedence over "rules and maxims." These necessities included not only "existing exigencies" but also "probable exigencies of the ages." And because probable exigencies were "illimitable," governing officials' powers had to be illimitable too.[25] Hamilton was convinced that a small governing elite was needed to create a new nation and then guide that nation to become a powerful player in world politics.

CONCLUSION

Fearful of disorder among men, concerned with crises that threatened the republic, and optimistic about opportunities on the horizon, most founders affirmed the need for a small governing elite to lead the nation. They reasoned as follows.

1. Men had a natural passion for distinction manifested in a manly quest for fame that elevated a few heroic men into the elite ranks of the natural aristocracy.
2. These select few men were portrayed as political patriarchs and father figures who could be trusted to exercise great power and still win men's consent.
3. They adhered to a code of political manhood that enjoined and enabled them to ignore public opinion, disregard law, and exercise political prerogative for the public good.
4. A small governing elite with extralegal powers was desperately needed to address the crises and realize the opportunities of the nation at a crucial historical turning point.

While the founders were fearful that powerful leaders could abuse their powers and deny men's liberty, they felt compelled to rely on a select few men to exhibit political manhood and exercise significant political powers for the public good.

This preference for powerful leadership created a problem that could not easily be ignored. The problem was that most American men were jealous of their liberty and many American men refused to recognize or legitimize the rule of ostensibly great leaders. Exactly who were these great leaders? The national consensus pretty much stopped at Benjamin Franklin and George Washington. Everyone else—including John Adams and Thomas Jefferson—faced vicious criticism and factional opposition. How far could the most qualified leader be trusted with substantial power? Some Americans were more prone to trust average family men to defend their rights than to rely on elites to avoid temptations toward tyranny.

If the founders considered America's male masses to be forces for public disorder, many American men considered the leaders who constituted a small governing elite to be vulnerable to political corruption. The founders were desperate to put American politics on a more stable footing than either radical democracy or aristocratic elitism would allow. We will see in the next chapter that the founders struck a compromise. They developed a theory of "weak citizenship" that invited family men's limited participation in politics and they developed a theory of "weak leadership" that called for gentlemen leaders to assume the everyday role of legislators and lawmakers. Many founders hoped that American politics would eventually become so routine and uneventful that it would no longer excite ordinary men's passions or feed ambitious leaders' cravings for power.

CHAPTER 6

Weak Citizens and Gentleman Legislators

Judith Sargent Murray worried that men's licentiousness, ignorance, and impudence generated a "tumultuous and up-rooting
hurricane" that threatened early America with "hell-born anarchy." She did not trust most (male) citizens to get too deeply involved in political life. Rather, she hoped that average family
men would defend liberty, exercise limited rights, and recognize
gradations among men, identify those in the higher ranks, elect
them to public office, and then render habitual obedience to
them.[1] Once most citizens cast their votes and chose their representatives, their political participation would be more or less fin-
ished until the next election cycle.

Which men were qualified to be representatives? Although
the founders sought great leaders to guide America through the
crisis of national birth and the achievement of national glory,
most founders did not expect heroic men to appear with any
regularity. They agreed with John Stevens, Jr., that, for the most
part, America should be governed by gentleman legislators who
first distinguished themselves in local politics, then worked their
way into state government, and eventually earned enough trust
and respect to gain national office.[2] Once in national office,
their main tasks were usually mundane, not momentous: they

were to make laws to protect men's rights and resolve men's conflicts peacefully.

Ultimately, most founders took a middle position on both citizenship and leadership. Caught between the revolutionary rhetoric of liberty and equality on the one hand and obsessive fears of disorderly men on the other, the founders struck a compromise by proposing a theory of weak citizenship. They focused citizen rights and responsibilities on military service and voting but not on public deliberation, instructions, decision making, and self-government. Caught between a desire for heroic leaders who were above the law and popular fears of corrupt politicians who abused the law, the founders engineered another compromise when they promoted a theory of weak leadership. America was to be governed by gentlemen legislators who were to enact laws and make policies intended to foster public order.

FAMILY MEN AND MILITARY SERVICE

The founders agreed that a key qualification for citizenship and a crucial exercise in citizenship was men's willingness to take up arms in defense of liberty, property, family, and nation. Could America's disorderly men be trusted to defend liberty? Not if they were selfish libertines who sought their own pleasure and refused to risk their health and wealth for the nation. Not if they were impulsive youths who were apt to avoid military duty or, failing that, desert their fellow soldiers. The founders put their confidence mainly in men who were husbands and fathers. Only family men could be trusted to fight against the nation's enemies because they alone had a family interest in protecting the liberty, property, and prosperity of the loved ones who would perpetuate their names and estates into the future.

The founders presumed that most family men would fight for the long-term good of their families and communities. In 1776 Thomas Paine promoted patriotism against what seemed like overwhelming British military and naval forces by reminding American men that their cause was not "the concern of a day, a year, or an age" but that their whole "posterity" was at stake.

The Revolution was not simply a battle for freedom and prosperity; it was a struggle for the freedom and prosperity of men's
wives and children, and their children's children too. Again in
1787 the founders invited American men to appreciate the importance of ratifying or refusing the U.S. Constitution by stress-
ing that their families and descendants would be affected by the
decision. Federalists and anti-federalists alike instructed citizens
to act "like men, like freemen and Americans, to transmit unimpaired to your latest posterity those rights, those liberties, which
have ever been so dear."[3] To act "like men" meant to be good
patriarchs who protected their families and estates by making responsible personal and political decisions.

Early American culture declared that a father's willingness to
take risks and make sacrifices for his family was natural. Any man
who had "the bowels of a father" felt compelled to defend his
children, their liberty, and their legacy. In turn, a father who
risked his health and life to defend his children's safety and future prospects was likely to be loved in life and fondly remembered at death. Nearly all Americans agreed that the one force in
life that was more powerful than men's egotistical desires for
self-preservation and self-gratification was their inherent drive
to protect and preserve their families and their posterity.[4]

The founders' experience was that men's commitment to
protect and preserve liberty, property, and family interests motivated them to teach their sons to bear arms and, when necessary,
to use their weapons to safeguard today's families and tomorrow's descendants. A responsible father urged and required his
sons to join the local militia and prove their manhood by exhibiting military bearing, martial skill, and battlefield courage. The
American militia muster became a sort of male family reunion
where fathers and sons along with uncles and nephews formed
the nucleus of local fighting forces. Many founders gloried at
the prospect of seeing sons enlist. John Adams wished that his
boys were old enough to serve in the Revolution. He wrote, "I
would send every one of them into the army in some capacity or
other. Military abilities and experience are a great advantage to

character."[5] Boys who risked their lives, served with honor, and survived their service emerged from the military as mature men and deserving citizens.

Of course, young men who went to war exposed themselves to disability and death. If they served with honor and died, they would be remembered with "recollections of manly sorrow" but their deaths would lop off future branches of their own family trees. That was why George Washington had mixed feelings about sending into battle one of his step-grandsons who was "the only male of his great great grandfather's family" and thus the sole hope for continuing his family line. Expecting war with France in 1798, Washington suggested that the boy enlist voluntarily. "If real danger threatened the country," he wrote, "no young man ought to be an idle spectator in its defense." However, Washington was hopeful that real danger would be averted. That way, the boy would "be entitled to the merit of proffered service without encountering the dangers of war" and he would likely live long enough to perpetuate his bloodline.[6]

Fathers who taught their sons to defend liberty, property, and family interests eventually had to let go of them. They had to allow their adult sons to grow up and exercise the manly freedom to acquire their own property, start their own families, and launch the next generation. A great many fathers resisted letting go. They wanted to keep their adult sons dependent as long as possible so they would continue to work on the family farm. Sometimes, they simply refused to give up their own paternal authority. Quite often, they used the prospect of a future inheritance to pressure adult sons into obeying them. Sooner or later, however, all fathers were expected to perform an act of manhood by renouncing their paternal authority and setting free their adult sons to achieve manly independence, family status, community standing, and citizenship.

FAMILY MEN AND CITIZENSHIP

The founders expected family patriarchs to be responsible and industrious. They were to govern their families with firm but loving authority, thereby controlling disorderly women and restraining disorderly female tendencies. Also, they were to work hard to ensure that all family members had adequate food, shelter, and clothing. Finally, they were to procreate posterity and devote themselves to promoting their children's welfare and future prospects. A worthy husband and responsible father measured up to manhood not only by serving in the local militia but also by demonstrating that he was man enough to support a family and achieve respectability in his community. Most founders felt that self-disciplined, responsible, and respectable family men had a sufficiently strong stake in the public good to be trusted with the basic rights of citizenship.

Eighteenth-century Americans inherited the traditional English belief that only substantial property owners, known as freeholders, were sufficiently independent and committed to the public good to qualify for citizenship. The American experience urged greater flexibility for several reasons. First, America's revolutionary rhetoric of liberty and equality broadcast the message that all men had a right to vote, serve on juries, and run for office. This radical rhetoric created a general presumption in favor of inclusive citizenship. Second, America's abundance of cheap, accessible land afforded nearly every young man a decent opportunity to acquire sufficient property to support a family. In America, most founders felt, virtually any young man could become a property owner and family patriarch. Although the founders continued to put property ownership at the center of citizenship, they began to associate men's family status with eligibility for citizenship.

Benjamin Franklin put it this way: "A man remarkably wavering and inconstant . . . can never be a truly useful member of the commonwealth." In Franklin's mind, a libertine or bachelor tended to act on passion and whim at the expense of the public good, whereas a family man by his marital status and responsibilities was "in the way of becoming a useful citizen." Even impoverished young men could "begin first as servants or journeymen, and if they are sober, industrious, and frugal, they soon become masters, establish themselves in business, marry, raise families, and become respectable citizens." Franklin's formula was straightforward: earned wealth was the basis for marriage; stable marriage was the foundation for fatherhood; responsible fatherhood gave a man an enduring stake in the public good; and a man's stake in public good motivated him to be a concerned, law-abiding citizen. Most founders considered a man's devotion to his family—especially to his "unborn posterity"—a powerful force for encouraging the sense of family responsibility and civic virtue essential to citizenship.[7]

The connection between men's family status and citizenship became a common theme in the founders' speeches and writings. In 1776, for example, Thomas Jefferson wrote, "I cannot doubt any attachment to his country in any man who has his family and [estate] in it." Jefferson advocated "extending the right of suffrage"—which he considered the most fundamental right of citizenship—to all family men. At the Constitutional Convention in 1787, fellow Virginian George Mason suggested that any man who headed a family was likely to have a strong enough concern for the public good to claim citizenship. Mason stated that the true idea of citizenship was that "every man having evidence of attachment to and permanent common interest with the society ought to share in all its rights and privileges." He suggested that "the parent of a number of children whose fortunes are to be pursued in his own country" should be considered a trustworthy person because his children were, in effect, guarantees of his patriotism. A family man would defend liberty, acquire property, support the public good, and obey the laws to ensure that his children would inherit liberty and property in a stable, law-abiding society.[8]

Some founders hinted at a more inclusive idea of family-based citizenship. Benjamin Franklin felt that "the sons of a substantial farmer," though not yet independent property owners or heads of their own families, anticipated becoming land-owning family men. They deserved the vote and "would not be pleased at being disfranchised." James Madison observed that America had "the precious advantage" of having a majority of "freeholders, or their heirs, or aspirants to freeholds."[9] Men who owned family estates, sons who were likely to inherit them, and even youths who aspired to acquire them conceivably could be trusted to combine manly independence and public loyalty to deserve the rights and responsibilities of citizenship.

In summary, many founders felt that average family men could be trusted to bear arms and vote in elections. It was an often-repeated remark that men's wives and children were "pledges of their fidelity" to social order, the public good, and national security. Their sense of family responsibility promoted the self-discipline and civic concern that enhanced the likelihood that they would act less as impassioned disorderly men and more as sober citizens who made reasonable and virtuous choices. Especially important, many founders felt, men's family status was a fundamental stimulus for them to obey laws and leaders in support of a stable public order.

OBEYING LAWS AND LEADERS

The founders sought to create a "government of laws." Their ideal republic was composed of citizens electing representatives who enacted laws that people habitually obeyed. Among the founders' greatest fears was that citizens would resist or refuse to obey their own representatives and legitimate laws whenever they felt obedience was inappropriate or inconvenient for them. For example, a libertine might vote in elections that produced legislators who, in turn, passed "white bastardy" laws that required the fathers of illegitimate children to pay child support. Few founders would have been surprised to learn that the same libertine would deny his paternity, refuse to support his offspring, denounce the laws, and condemn the government that attempted to enforce them. How was it possible to create a government of laws when so many men seemed to treat laws as inapplicable to them?

Family status was an important part of the answer. Many founders felt that America's family men were likely to obey laws that were enacted by legislators who headed their own families. Why? Fathers who disciplined themselves and made sacrifices to promote their children's prospects were likely to recognize that politicians who also were family men had a strong incentive to enact only laws that were likely to have a positive effect on their own wives, children, and posterity. Families were pledges both of citizens' fidelity and politicians' integrity. Even a corrupt legislator was likely to hesitate before approving burdensome taxes that might oppress his own family and descendants along with everyone else. Most founders felt that the greater the trust binding family men who were citizens to politicians who also were family men, the more likely it was that family men would obey most laws—even when obedience seemed to be unwarranted to them.

When opponents of the U.S. Constitution argued that the proposed national government would be tyrannical, defenders of the Constitution responded that the new national government would be trustworthy because it would be staffed by public officials who also were family men. For instance, John Jay tried to dispel oppositional fears that the President and Senate would ratify treaties contrary to the public good by asserting that government officials "and their family estates will . . . be equally bound and affected with the rest of the community." James Iredell hoped to reduce oppositional fears that the Constitution's unification of taxing powers and military authority was dangerous by arguing that it was improbable that politicians would destroy "themselves, their families, and fortunes, even if they have no regard to their public duty." Zachariah Johnston sought to refute oppositional fears that a legislator would enact unjust taxes by pointing out that a family-oriented politician would not want to act in ways likely to bring suffering to "his own posterity."[10] Those founders advocating ratification of the U.S. Constitution commonly claimed that family men who were citizens could trust and would obey family men who served as lawmakers.

Many founders felt that fatherhood formed a psychic bond fostering mutual trust among citizens and public authorities. The average family man was apt to identify with paternalistic public officials. A father who would not make rash decisions that endangered his children had good reason to expect that a politician who also was a father would not seek "the precarious enjoyment of rank and power" by participating in "a system which would reduce his . . . posterity to slavery and ruin." Fathers who were citizens and politicians who were fathers shared a cautious approach to the future. Equally important, both agreed on the value of patriarchal authority. A family father governed his household to ensure the welfare of his children. He was likely to identify with a government official who committed himself to serving as a public father figure who "watch[ed] over the whole with paternal care and affection."[11] This conjuncture of fatherhood and national politics made the new government feel familiar, appear friendly, and seem legitimate. It merited and attracted men's obedience to the laws.

In summary, the founders believed that most family men could be trusted to claim the rights of citizenship, defend liberty, and comply with the laws enacted by their elected public officials. This broad trust in family men as citizens, in turn, narrowed the founders' potential for associating women with citizenship. Women could never be family men. Thus, women could not base their claims to citizenship on a father's long-term commitment to the public good. Nor could women be expected to have a father's appreciation for, trust in, or predisposition to obey politicians who were themselves fathers or father figures. Norms of manhood and qualifications for citizenship came wrapped in a single package. That was why the founding generation had to devise a whole new language (republican womanhood) simply to contemplate female citizenship. Even then, few founders actually contemplated it and nearly all agreed that wives, mothers, and daughters should be excluded from the militia muster and the polling place.

WEAK CITIZENSHIP

The founders' trust in family men as a citizens was discernible. It is important to note, however, that their trust was also quite limited. Family men were still flawed creatures. They often failed to restrain their passions (e.g., adultery), fulfill their family responsibilities (e.g., abandonment), or reconcile their family interests with the public good (e.g., military desertion). Aware that some husbands and fathers such as western Massachusetts farmers defended their family estates by rebelling against their governors or Philadelphia artisans protected their family interests by disobeying elite authorities, the founders recognized that sober family men sometimes disobeyed the laws, committed crimes, fueled mob actions, and fomented public disorder. They sought security against what they considered family men's lapses in good behavior. That security took the form of "weak citizenship."

The founders experimented with two versions of citizenship. The framers of the 1776 Pennsylvania state constitution acted on a theory of strong citizenship. They believed that citizens should have maximal access to public information, deliberate with other citizens, and determine the best course of action. They should elect representatives, regularly rotate them in and out of office, instruct them to vote or act in mandated ways, and provide them with the appropriate institutional means (such as a one-house legislature) to translate public preferences directly into laws and public policy. From their vantage point, average family men could be trusted to govern themselves. They were an intelligent, participatory citizenry that should make public decisions and then use their elected officials to express, tally, record, and administer their public preferences.

By contrast, the framers of the U.S. Constitution in 1787 acted on a theory of weak citizenship. They gave citizens three important but restricted tasks. One was to serve in the militia when called to do so by their leaders. The second citizenship responsibility was to cast ballots every few years, hopefully, for virtuous and talented representatives who would rely on their own consciences, experience, reason, and will to deliberate and make public decisions. Third, citizens were expected to comply with their leaders' decisions, most importantly, by habitually obeying the laws. All in all, the idea of weak citizenship suggested that family men's primary political task was not to participate in self-government; rather it was to elect and obey the governing elite.

Most founders did not subscribe to the theory of strong citizenship. They feared that American men would want to participate in untried schemes of self-government, perhaps capture control of the national government, and then use it as an instrument to deprive wealthy individuals of their property rights or to undertake other foolish actions certain to cause serious public disorder. One crucial reason why many founders favored ratification of the U.S. Constitution was that it fragmented the national government by instituting devices such as the separation of powers, federalism, checks and balances, staggered elections, direct and indirect elections, and explicit prohibitions against government intervention in individual lives and state politics. Fragmentation functioned as an insurance policy. Even if an impassioned majority of men got deeply involved in politics and captured control of several major sectors of the national government, political fragmentation ensured that the power of a tyrannical majority to foment disorder still would be minimal.

In any one national election, for example, a mass movement of citizens might win control of the House of Representatives. However, it could accomplish very little if the President, the Senate majority, or the Supreme Court chose to neutralize it. Once citizens recognized that it was all but impossible for an impassioned majority or an impulsive mob to control and manipulate the national government, they were apt to become less interested in national politics and more focused on their own family fortunes. According to the theory of weak citizenship, it was a good thing for most men to ignore politics most of the time. That way they would leave lawmaking and public policy to their more experienced and talented representatives.

A crucial exception to the founders' fragmentation of the national government should be noted. The U.S. Constitution gave the president nearly unchecked power to command the nation's military forces. On his word alone he could order out the national army and take command of the state militia to put down domestic disorders or fend off foreign threats. President Washington set a precedent for presidential command over the national means of violence in the 1790s when he used military force to defeat a Pennsylvania tax protest known as the Whiskey Rebellion. Ultimately, the national government was not particularly useful to common men who sought a system of democratic self-government, but it was quite serviceable to government elites who wanted to secure public order.

I can now be more precise about the founders' faith in family men as trustworthy citizens. The founders felt that ordinary family men were qualified to be *part-time* citizens. The founders expected average family men to spend most of their time cultivating their farms, governing their wives, providing for their children, and contributing to their communities. Their daily existence would center on family, farm, and friends. By contrast, ordinary family men's participation in politics would be peripheral to everyday life. It involved episodic mustering with the militia, occasional jury duty, and periodic voting for representatives. Most founders felt that this mixture of strong family-centered life and weak citizenship was the best formula for keeping otherwise disorderly men preoccupied with private productive activities rather than invested in destructive public conflicts.

THE GENTLEMAN ELITE

After the Revolution, many founders felt it was especially important to keep men preoccupied with productive family activity rather than politics. It seemed as if men's revolutionary self-sacrifice and patriotism were transformed into postwar selfishness, materialism, and greed. Some founders resigned themselves to the inevitability of male selfishness, but most founders urged American men to exhibit greater self-restraint and civic concern. In 1783, for example, General Washington instructed demobilizing soldiers to engage in "wise and manly conduct" by showing "conciliating dispositions" toward other men.[12] Military courage bound soldier to soldier on the battlefield. Perhaps self-discipline, good morals and manners, and sociable behavior could bind men together in the new republic. The founders called for more civility among the citizenry.

Civility was the master virtue of gentlemen. Benjamin Franklin explained that a gentleman was always "searching for and seizing every opportunity to serve and oblige" other men. Franklin made it his own rule "to forbear all direct contradiction to the sentiments of others and all positive assertion of my own." Civility made him a more pleasant companion. It also increased the likelihood that other men would respect him, listen to him, and perhaps agree with him. Thomas Jefferson applauded Franklin's advice and then added his own belief that politeness, good manners, and mild flattery usually gratified and conciliated other men. Those who practiced these gentlemanly virtues gained the "good will" of others and helped to preserve "peace and tranquillity" among men.[13] Civility contributed to public order.

The founders generally approved of men who cultivated civility as a means to move up the social ladder. They saw social climbing as a virtue. It invited ordinary family men to emulate respectable gentlemen and solicit their esteem in order to be admitted to their ranks. An effective social climber repressed his disorderly animal instincts and exemplified the refined morals and manners of "civilized" beings. If "a man without taste and the acquirements of genius" was no better than an "orangutan," *The United States Magazine* suggested, a man who studied courtesy books and mastered the details of graceful speech, genteel conduct, appropriate dress, and other social subtleties could transform himself into a refined gentleman of merit.[14]

One of the recognized duties of refined gentlemen was to serve as benefactors to men who were lower down the social ladder. Gentlemen were expected to be friendly to their "inferiors" and show respect to all men who were "below" them. Gentlemen were supposed to "defend and patronize" lesser men and serve as role models and teachers to them. Thus, they had an obligation to do their best to reform coarse, rough-hewn men by encouraging them to achieve manhood through refined manners and civil conduct. John Adams asserted that gentlemen had a positive duty to spread among commoners "good humor, sociability, good manners, and good morals . . . some politeness but more civility."[15]

Although the founders praised and promoted civility among all classes of men, they actually expected relatively few men to cultivate it or truly excel at it. The problem for most men was that they suffered from disorderly passions that prevented them from appreciating the benefits of civility or from practicing it with any degree of regularity. Indeed, even highly refined men from the best families and foremost educational institutions often failed to exhibit good manners. In 1797, for example, Thomas Jefferson was particularly appalled by U.S. Senators who were so heated in their political debates that, outside the Senate, they crossed the street to avoid crossing paths with their rivals, or they insultingly turned their heads to avoid tipping their hats at them. "This may do for young men with whom passion is enjoyment," Jefferson commented, "but it is afflicting to peaceable minds." An accomplished gentleman did not contribute to social friction and political faction. He acted on conscience and always sought to make friends with adversaries.[16]

The modest class of men who mastered the high art of civility constituted the America's gentleman elite. Mastery was a complex matter. Like all mature men, gentlemen attained and maintained manly independence. They displayed "a free and manly spirit." They thought with boldness, energy, and creativity. They formed their own principles and acted on conscience. The founders felt that relatively few men achieved a high degree of independence or sustained it when pressured to conform to society's prevailing opinions. Even more challenging, gentlemen exhibited a capacity to balance manly independence with civility. They had to stand their moral ground without offending other men. A gentlemen combined "manly candor" with a "manly tone of intercourse" in order to deal "freely" with another man and treat him "like a friend." Many founders admired Edmund Randolph for his ability to combine independent manhood and social civility. Under extremely trying circumstances, Randolph refused to make "an unmanly sacrifice" of his own judgment, took an unpopular position on an important issue, but still paid homage to his critics and sought to befriend them.[17] The founders praised men who acted decisively without alienating others because they were especially qualified to be political leaders who assumed responsibility for maintaining public order.

WEAK LEADERSHIP

We saw in the previous chapter that the founders focused on heroic leaders when great crises or historic opportunities were at stake. Simultaneously, they recognized that the daily affairs of government were rather routine. Legislators dwelled on the minutiae of lawmaking. Executives focused on the particulars of administration. Judges dealt in the details of law. Heroes were neither available nor needed for everyday politics. Members of the gentleman elite would do just fine.

Few founders expected or desired average family men to hold leadership positions in government. Instead, historian Gordon Wood writes, "they expected that the sons of such humble or ungenteel men, if they had abilities, would . . . rise into the ranks of gentlemen and become eligible for high political office."[18] The founders hoped for and even applauded the social climbing of commoners who made it into the gentleman elite which was, in turn, the main recruitment pool for national political leadership. Why?

The founders associated important virtues with members of the gentleman elite. They had "the most attractive merit and the most diffusive and established characters" which qualified them for political leadership in three ways. First, gentlemen were independent enough to make conscientious decisions but civil enough to act "in conjunction with others." This combination of manly virtues enabled them to build "endearing ties of gratitude and love which unite man to man." Second, gentlemen exhibited "exemplary morals, great patience, calmness, coolness, and attention." They were men of great "knowledge, wisdom, and prudence" but they were also men of great "mercy and compassion." They were qualified to govern because they mastered the rationality necessary for making law and the tenderness needed to administer it with fairness and flexibility. Third, gentlemen were known for their "exemplary conduct." Their morals and manners were "contagious." They provided a "shining example" of manhood and civility to lesser men. They were qualified leaders because they were role-models who encouraged their followers to be better men and better citizens.[19]

The founders believed that gentlemen exhibited a combination of manly virtues that fostered greater unity, harmony, and civility in public life. They were especially qualified for positions of political leadership because they had a capacity to maintain and manage public order. They were not political heroes who acted regardless of public opinion and law; they were not political heroes who exercised political prerogative to resolve major crises; and they were not political heroes who assumed extralegal powers to found new nations, write innovative constitutions, or achieve national greatness. Quite the contrary, gentlemen legislators were comparatively weak leaders with modest goals. Their main tasks were to solicit, soothe, and educate public opinion and to make laws, honor and obey them, and encourage all Americans to do the same. Overall, gentleman legislators were qualified to administer government competently and gain the compliance of common citizens.

Most founders felt that the main obstacle to mundane government by gentleman legislators was not leaders' tendency to usurp power. Rather, it was citizens' tendency to confuse true gentleman legislators and deceitful demagogues. The founders often warned citizens to beware of the political pretenders in their midst. Voters had to learn to distinguish between gentlemen of "real worth" who were qualified to govern and the "popularity-seeker, or mere man of the people" who "banishes candor and substitutes prejudice." Voters also needed to separate the gentleman legislator who merited the "esteem of the virtuous and wise" from the disorderly factional leader who engaged himself in a "mad pursuit of low popularity" rather than the public good.[20]

Unfortunately, most founders feared, citizens could be deceived and often were deceived by silver-tongued demagogues who lured them down the path of disruptive behavior. Popular novels and political narratives expressed the idea that even responsible husbands, fathers, citizens, and patriots were vulnerable to being duped by pretenders. That was why it was crucial that real gentlemen establish and protect their reputations. They needed to ensure that citizens invest their confidence in truly worthy leaders and mark their ballots for them alone.

REPUTABLE LEADERS

Colonial Americans considered "a good name" of great importance. A man had to establish and maintain a "reputation of being worthy of belief or trust" to participate in the oral agreements that shaped most economic and social interactions. The great significance of reputation lasted into the founding era when, for example, Martin Howard proclaimed "the high value of a good name and how dear it is to men of sentiment and honor." A good name fortified a man's self-esteem, enhanced his economic opportunities, increased his admirers, and enabled him to rise into the ranks of true gentlemen. A good name also provided a man with friends who would defend him against "the assassin who stabs reputation."[21]

Most American founders were obsessed with what other men said or wrote about them. Early in the Revolution, for instance, George Washington suffered heightened anxiety that his reputation would "fall" if he continued his military command with too few soldiers only to be charged with incompetence, or if he resigned his military command only to be criticized for disloyalty to his country. Washington complained about the "impossibility of serving with reputation" and instructed his cousin Lund Washington to defend his character. Most founders considered politicians' devotion to reputation a good thing. Citizens were likely to trust public officials whose concern for their reputations guarded them against "undue influence." Politicians were unlikely to sink into corruption so long as they feared "the censure of the people."[22]

Some founders considered a man's reputation nearly as important as life itself. One reason was personal. Benjamin Franklin suggested that "It is so natural to wish to be well spoken of, whether alive or dead." Judith Sargent Murray's fictional narrator, "The Gleaner," put reputation at the very center of men's lives and deaths when he declared: "I would be distinguished and respected by my contemporaries; I would be continued on grateful remembrance when I make my exit; and I would descend with celebrity to posterity."[23] Reputation determined how a man would be remembered by his family, progeny, and all posterity.

Ideally, men's concern for their reputations helped to keep their conduct within the boundaries of good behavior. For example, many neutrals and Tories stayed in their communities during the American Revolution. They learned to speak and act with great restraint in order to maintain just enough respectability to insulate themselves from the anger, humiliation, and physical punishments meted out by patriots. Meanwhile, those patriots who aspired to become public leaders had to establish good civic reputations to gain the respect and deference of friends, neighbors, and supporters who otherwise treasured their manly independence and maintained significant skepticism toward leadership authority. A potential leader's good reputation could neutralize public fears of future political betrayals.

The founders saw reputation as a significant bond between citizens and leaders. For instance, Charles Pinckney thought that most citizens would trust leaders who "connect the tie of property with that of reputation." Noah Webster felt that most American men would place their confidence in officials whose jealousy of their reputations was a "guarantee" that they would faithfully discharge their public duties. Pelatiah Webster was convinced that most ambitious politicians were likely to earn "public confidence" when their concern for their "personal reputations with all the eyes of the world on them" induced them to exhibit "noble, upright, and worthy behavior." To summarize to this point, the founders felt that most men failed to excel at manly candor and civility; but they also believed that most men admired and obeyed gentleman leaders who were reputed to merit public esteem. Annis Boudinot Stockton translated this idea into the language of manhood when she suggested that "the free born" would resign their "native rights" only to *"Men."*[24]

PRIVILEGED SONS

The founders excluded all women from citizenship and leadership positions regardless of their virtues and reputations, and they provided most white males with limited opportunities to ascend into the gentleman elite and gain national political office. Although the founders did express the belief that all talented white males were eligible for admission into the gentleman elite and political leadership, they were actually quite wary about admitting untried newcomers to high political positions. Indeed, they preferred to privilege their own sons in the competition for social acceptance and government employment.

The founders recognized that women, like men, could practice civility and achieve elevated reputations. Many founders felt that women outdid men in exhibiting refined morals and manners as well as in conciliating other people. Several leaders even hinted that women's accomplishments qualified them for leadership positions. Thomas Paine was hopeful that some "Jersey maid" would emulate Joan of Arc and "spirit up her country-men" to win the Revolution. Judith Sargent Murray asserted that women's refinement and leadership abilities were unsur-passed by men. Still, Paine and Murray depicted women as second-class leaders. Paine's Jersey maid mostly shamed recalci-trant men into combat; and Murray's female leaders mostly mo-tivated male warriors to fight. At best, the founders saw female leaders as auxiliaries to the republic rather than as citizens and statesmen of the republic.[25]

Could any white male climb the social ladder into the ranks of gentlemen and from there rise into positions of political author-ity? The founders approved of young men of modest means who exhibited personal merit by cultivating manly virtues and talents to achieve prosperity and perform public service. Writers often used Benjamin Franklin as a noteworthy example of the "self-made man" who transformed a meager family legacy into a sub-stantial estate and memorable diplomatic career. The founding generation regularly instructed young males to emulate Frank-lin and "show yourselves men." They also honored the "self-made, industrious men" who they located at the heart and soul of national independence and prosperity.[26]

The founders usually complemented their approval of self-made men with widespread support for equal political opportu-nity. John Stevens, Jr. put it this way:

No government that has ever yet existed in the world affords so ample a field to individuals of all ranks for the display of political talents and abilities. . . . No man who has real merit, let his situation be what it will, need despair. He first distinguishes himself amongst his neighbors and township and country meeting; he is next sent to the state legislature. In this theater his abilities, whatever they are, are exhibited in their true colors, and displayed to the views of every man in the state; from hence his ascent to a seat in Congress. . . . Such a regular uninterrupted gra-dation from the chief men in a village to the chair of the President of the United States, which this government affords to all her citizens without distinction, is a perfection in republican government hereto-fore unknown.[27]

American politics provided tiered tests to separate less deserving men from the gentleman elite qualified to govern other men.

Simultaneously, most founders were willing to compromise the norm of equal political opportunity by attaching special advantages to father-son family ties. The founders generally believed that nature and upbringing fortified father-son bonds. Thomas Jefferson wrote, "Experience proves that the moral and physical qualities of man, whether good or evil, are transmissible from father to son." Although a virtuous father could sire evil sons, he was more likely to produce virtuous ones. John Adams agreed that "Wise men beget fools, and honest men knaves; but these instances . . . are not general. If there is often a likeness in figure and feature, there is generally more in mind and heart." Accordingly, when a father achieved a reputation for being a worthy gentleman and public leader, most men rightfully presumed that his sons merited the same esteem. The result was that an eminent man's son had a distinct political advantage (over youths of more humble origins). Most men were predisposed "to honor the memory of his father, to congratulate him as the successor to his estate, and frequently to complement him with elections to the offices he held." What Adams called "family spirit" helped to promote family-based political dynasties.[28]

Furthermore, it was common practice among the founders to provide the sons of gentleman colleagues or political friends with letters of introduction to other influential members of social and political elites. These letters usually highlighted both young men's family standing and their individual merit. For example, Thomas Jefferson introduced Mr. Lyons to John Adams as a "son of one of our judges" and "a sensible worthy young physician." He recommended Mr. Rutledge to Adams by writing, "Your knowledge of his father will introduce him to your notice. He merits it moreover on his own account."[29] Members of the gentleman elite regularly guided their sons (as well as

_ .er gentlemen's sons) into social relationships and employment opportunities that were advantageous to privileged young men's economic, social, and political prospects.

The founders did not provide gentlewomen access to citizenship status or leadership positions. They held out to white family men the promise of weak citizenship and government by gentleman legislators. They opened avenues of political opportunity to talented young white males but they also continued to privilege their own sons by networking them into the gentleman elite and giving them exceptional access to the nation's power brokers and positions of political power.

CONCLUSION

The founders supported weak citizenship and gentleman legislators for the following reasons.

1. Family men could be trusted with citizenship because they would defend liberty, devote themselves to the public good, obey laws, and trust other family men who served as leaders.
2. However, family men were prone to lapse from orderly behavior. At best, they merited a weak citizenship limited mainly to military service and voting for representatives.
3. Public officials were expected to come from the ranks of gentlemen who excelled at the manly independence necessary for leadership and the manly civility essential to ensuring order among citizens.
4. Every (male) citizen had an opportunity to rise into the ranks of gentleman legislators, but young men with elite family connections were privileged in the competition for social acceptance and political power.

Few founders imagined building a republic in which the majority of men ruled themselves; some founders fantasized about a republic ruled by a few heroic leaders; but most founders promoted among white family men a version of weak citizenship that limited participation and fostered obedience to gentleman legislators.

Did the founders expect the gap between weak citizens and gentleman legislators to close over time? James Madison considered the possibility of greater circulation and growing trust between citizens and leaders. He suggested that the average voter was likely to become more sophisticated when participating in elections. His views would be refined and enlarged. A more sophisticated citizenry would likely recognize and defeat demagogues and other pretenders while bringing forth from its own ranks new generations of gentleman legislators. Eventually, voters would develop a "manly confidence" in public officials who were drawn from the common people but "particularly distinguished" among them.[30]

Madison thought this manly confidence which united ordinary citizens and their leaders would be reinforced by Constitutional guarantees that legislators could "make no law which will not have its full operation on themselves and their friends as well as on the great mass of society." He called this one of "the strongest bonds by which human policy can connect the rulers and people together." Alexander Hamilton concurred. The principle that legislators and citizens were obliged to obey the same laws sounded "true and . . . strong chords of sympathy between the representative and the constituent."[31] Hopefully, fears of men's erratic passions and leaders' potential corruption could be reduced by a fraternal agreement that, ordinarily, citizens and leaders would play by the same rules.

I suggested in Part One that the gendering of American politics began with a compromise between traditional patriarchal ideals and emerging republican norms that resulted in the doctrine of republican womanhood. Women were formally excluded from citizenship and leadership but were nevertheless expected to position themselves in families to exercise informal public influence in the new republic. In Part Two, I suggested that the gendering of American politics was concluded by a second compromise. The founders often expressed the desire to exclude disorderly men from politics (Chapter 4) and empower a heroic few men to exercise great political prerogative (Chapter 5) but they generally settled for granting weak citizenship to white family men and supporting elite government by gentleman legislators (Chapter 6). Even with this compromise, the male majority was subordinated to a political elite.

The founding era did not settle the battle between the sexes or competition within the ranks of men. The emergence of republican womanhood proved to be a prelude to important nineteenth- and twentieth-century struggles for women's rights. The subordination of most men by exclusion or by weak citizenship set the stage for centuries of ongoing struggle for greater popular democracy against elite government. The gendering of American politics during the founding era proved to be a legacy that was addressed and contested by future generations of Americans. We now turn to that legacy.

The Founders' Legacy

CHAPTER 7

America's Gendered Politics

The American founders' gendered politics was challenged and changed in the next two hundred years. American women acquired parental primacy, gained access to higher education, won property rights, secured suffrage, and moved into the military, jury boxes, and elective and appointed political offices. Formerly excluded males such as poor whites, African Americans, and Irish Catholics achieved political recognition, citizenship, and public office. Meanwhile, democratic activists forged populist movements intended to enhance citizen decision making and erode elite authority. The American founders' legacy of patriarchal politics was continuously contested.

But it was not eliminated. Virtually every historical struggle against patriarchal politics was opposed by large numbers of Americans who feared that change would generate great public disorder. For example, antifeminists regularly argued that women's political rights would destroy families and produce public chaos. Skeptics of political inclusiveness often asserted that poor men and minority men were too impassioned and irrational to be trusted with citizenship. Local and national elites also criticized democratic activism as an invitation to mob rule. Long after the founding, American men's rule over women and elite men's domination of other men continued to attract significant support.

As we enter the twenty-first century, patriarchal politics still attracts significant support. The founders' identification of womanhood with domesticity as the only appropriate basis for women's public influence remains a powerful factor in American politics. The founders' fear of disorderly men, limited trust in family men, and reliance on governing elites still pervade American politics. It is fair to say that the founders' gendering of American politics has proven to be remarkably resilient.

NINETEENTH-CENTURY DOMESTICITY

Nineteenth-century American writers perpetuated the founders' attachment to female domesticity. They believed that home life was more natural and desirable for women than public life. They even suggested that middle-class women were privileged to be able to stay at home where they could cultivate religion, practice female craft traditions, and build intimate relationships while avoiding the vice and corruption associated with men's economic dealings and governmental affairs. Popular magazines and guidebooks advised women that female self-fulfillment was rooted in home life and reproduction. Women who fully appreciated their natural cycles of menstruation, pregnancy, lactation, and menopause would be rewarded with feelings of accomplishment and happiness.

The middle-class American women who bought into this "cult of domesticity" were expected to exemplify virtue and piety, redeem their husbands from vices such as idleness, intemperance, gambling, and adultery, and serve as full-time mothers who raised productive, law-abiding children. They would be busy women with no time for frailty, foolishness, or ineptitude. Advocates of female domesticity, or "real womanhood," insisted on female education to enhance women's effectiveness as wives and mothers. They also urged women to develop job skills to enhance family prosperity. Domestic women were to be educated, active, accomplished women.

They also were to be influential women who exercised leverage over their husbands. When marriages were based on love,
women gained emotional influence over men. They could withhold or give affection to control their mates. Women's emotional influence was enhanced by an emerging "ideology of
passionlessness." Whereas eighteenth-century men expressed
fears of unrestrained female sexuality, nineteenth-century men
reversed course and questioned whether women had any sex
drive at all. Physicians suggested that women had dull libidos
and fragile bodies. Too much sex was harmful to them. This ideology of passionlessness positioned wives to budget sex (to say
"no" with authority), use the threat of withholding sex to control their husbands' conduct, and practice a sufficient degree of
sexual abstinence to avoid an adulthood consumed by childbearing and child-rearing.[2] ~~Women started to take control~~

Additionally, nineteenth-century American women garnered
influence by gaining recognition as primary parents. With more
fathers working away from home and most mothers honored for
domesticity, mainstream Americans came to believe that only
mothers "had the power to transform malleable infants into
moral, productive adults." The ideal mother acquired an education that enriched her parenting skills. She assumed management of family resources to shape a proper home environment
for her children. And she demanded her husband's acquiescence
to maternal child rearing techniques. By mid-century, a New
York court could rule: "All other things being equal, the mother
is the most proper parent to be entrusted with the custody of a
child."[3] Maternal authority was on the rise.

Domestic women also gained some leverage in the family
economy. Middle-class women were more than homemakers
who provided their husbands a place to rest and recuperate after
the travails of the marketplace. Women performed essential labor. They cooked, clothed, and fed their families, served as
front-line care givers and medical providers, engaged in household manufacturing and maintenance, and much, much
more—all of which augmented many husbands' otherwise in-

adequate incomes. This non-wage labor did not provide women an independent economic identity; however, it often enabled domestic women to have significant say in their families' economic decisions.

Unquestionably, domestic women's status and leverage increased in the nineteenth century—but always within limits. For example, women's idealized cultural portrayal as "angels of the house" legitimized their moral authority at home but it also justified assigning them responsibility for nearly all public problems. Nineteenth-century critics pointed to wives' failings as the main source of their husbands' vices. They cited mothers' mistakes as the primary reason for delinquent boys' drinking, gambling, and whoring. "If only women were better wives and mothers," a common complaint went, "Americans would suffer less grief, poverty, crime, and disorder." Meanwhile, women who left their homes to take paying jobs in the marketplace were deemed doubly guilty, first for abandoning their domestic responsibilities and second for participating in the public world of male vices.

Domestic women's moral elevation and family influence also remained restricted. The nineteenth-century marriage contract was not an agreement between equals. Partners were more or less free to choose their mates but they were not free to negotiate marital roles and responsibilities. Instead, spousal rights and duties were regulated by traditional patriarchal laws that continued to presume that wives were their husbands' dependents and subordinates. Judges not only enforced female dependency and subordination; they also played the role of substitute family patriarchs when husbands and fathers failed to fulfill their family responsibilities. Meanwhile, men's monopoly of cultural, economic, political, military, and legal power guaranteed that men retained the authority to set patriarchal limits to women's influence within their homes and beyond them.

WOMEN CIVILIZING MEN

Nineteenth-century advice books counseled women to keep their husbands from "rough companions, bars, or gambling halls" and to contribute to "softening and refining the society." Educational writer Catherine Beecher went further. She urged women to use feminine influence over fathers, husbands, and sons to improve America. Women's elevated moral stature and emotional leverage were forces "to which [men] will yield not only willingly but proudly." Female forces were sufficiently powerful to control "the destinies of a nation." Other writers suggested that wives performed a great public service when they sought to improve husbands' "moral feelings" and "spiritual nature." Literary figures such as Ralph Waldo Emerson and Nathaniel Hawthorne agreed that domestic women were essential for civilizing disorderly men.[4]

Most Americans believed that women's greatest influence for good occurred when they nursed and nurtured a new and better breed of men. Ideally, mothers created domestic environments marked by an honest simplicity that fostered male moral regeneration. Ideally, mothers acted as ethical exemplars who put selflessness above selfishness, preferred frugality to sensuality, substituted cooperation for competition, and elevated affection above conflict. Ideally, mothers taught their boys to discipline unruly passions, practice civility, and ultimately choose productivity, marriage, and family responsibility. Influential mothers were to devote much of their lives to curing male licentiousness.

Women's curative mission became a common justification for extending women's educational opportunities and admitting women into caring professions such as teaching. Approaching the end of the nineteenth century, middle-class women began to claim that they could refine their "maternal sensitivity, moral superiority, and domestic ability" by participating in private literary clubs and by extending their maternal influence into public life. If educated, activist women could civilize their husbands and sons at home, they also could reform the male rogues, gamblers, drinkers, thieves, deceivers, and bullies who monopolized the marketplace and corrupted the nation's political system. Women could become the public housekeepers of America.[5]

The mere possibility that women would use domesticity as a justification for participating in public life generated a mixed reaction. On the one hand, critics resurrected traditional patriarchal arguments that women in public abandoned their families and associated themselves with disorderly male activities. Critics also sounded an alarm against spreading "Momism," contending that women were becoming too influential, too powerful, both at home and in society. Women dominated their husbands, emasculated their sons, effeminized public education, promoted welfare dependency, and made American males unfit for the rigors of economic competition and political adversity. According to critics, the result of all of this female mischief was a new generation of effeminate boys who needed to be separated from women and exposed to forces of remasculinization—which might include roughing it in nature, participating in organized sports, and undergoing the rigors of military training.

On the other hand, the idea of extending women's domestic influence into public life was attractive to governing elites that were concerned with promoting and protecting public order. Women reformers supported religious revivals, moral purity campaigns, Sabbath Schools, child welfare, charity, and public education as manifestations of maternal caring and sources of public stability. They protested against prostitution, gambling, and intemperance as seedbeds for male crime, family destruction, and public disorder. The women's temperance movement, the women's club movement, and the women's settlement house movement all sought to organize mothers to spread morality, make men into better husbands and fathers, and make cities more habitable and harmonious. Female reformers wanted to civilize men and stabilize public life.

Male elites wanted the same things. Consequently, they lent support to female reform movements that promised to foster among men greater "individual comportment, self-restraint, and social order." They applauded women's public efforts to get male workers to swear off "idleness, profanity, and intemperance" and strive to "move up the ladder of success." They especially cheered the women's temperance movement because they believed that worker sobriety minimized labor conflict and prevented strikes. Leading clergymen, capitalists, politicians, and military brass encouraged female reformers who "tidied up the man's world."[6]

However, America's female reformers and male elites parted company over the issue of women's *political* power. Many female reformers included among their goals not only improving women's private lives but also enhancing women's political influence. For example, women's club activists argued that mothers should have a right to vote in school board elections and hold office on school boards. Some activists suggested that mothers also should have the right to deliberate and legislate on a range of local and national family issues. Other female reformers went further. They proposed that America move toward a "maternal commonwealth" that encouraged women's full participation in politics and promoted women's cooperative morality rather than men's cut-throat competition as a better basis for government.[7] Perceiving politicized women as an added source of public disorder, male elites mostly resisted women's claims to partial as well as to full citizenship.

WOMEN'S SUFFRAGE

Nineteenth-century Americans continued the founders' practice of identifying female domesticity as the basis for women's civic contributions. "Home," wrote one Mrs. Graves, "is the cradle of the human race. . . . It is here [a woman] can best serve her country, by training up good citizens, just, humane, and enlightened legislators."[8] Civic leaders still instructed American mothers to raise public-spirited sons and then relinquish them to defend the nation and to start their own families. The belief that women's primary public service was to bear children and rear patriotic sons endured well into the twentieth century.

Simultaneously, nineteenth-century Americans began to express the more modern idea that women as well as men were born free and equal and could be governed only with their own consent. The conviction that women had natural rights and deserved citizenship provided a moral foundation for women's struggle for political equality. Nineteenth-century feminists rewrote the Declaration of Independence to include women. They claimed civil, economic, and political rights for women. And they devoted more than a half-century to winning voting rights for women. Suffragists (activists for women's voting rights) argued that women were independent, rational human beings and proud, patriotic Americans who deserved the full rights and responsibilities of citizenship.

Early feminist activists such as Elizabeth Cady Stanton and Susan B. Anthony promoted images of independent womanhood only to evoke patriarchal fears among the opposition. Opponents of women's suffrage warned that politicized women would forsake their families and partake in disorderly public conduct. Orestes Brownson was especially fearful that independent women would care more about themselves than their families. They would fail to make the sacrifices necessary to civilize their husbands and raise virtuous sons. Instead, they would attempt to use politics for their own self-serving reasons.[9] New female disorders would add to current male disorders, and the politics of greed and conflict would undermine the politics of the public good.

Suffragists formulated two major responses. One response was that both sexes had the same God-given, natural rights to participate in politics, choose their representatives, and serve the public. Furthermore, there was no good reason to believe that women's political participation, choices, and service would be any more disruptive than men's exercise of citizenship. Both sexes were capable of acting on the basis of virtue and reason. The second response was that voting women were likely to reduce if not cure male licentiousness and excess in politics. For example, Isabella Hooker assured Americans that enfranchised women would enter the polling place carrying "the God-given power of womanhood—of motherhood." Her case for "maternal suffrage" was that female domesticity wed to women's voting rights would elevate the moral tone of public discourse and produce improved laws and policies that emphasized compassion, caring, and integrity over male greed, power hunger, and corruption. Voting women would restore civic virtue to American politics.[10]

American women enhanced their claims to citizenship by engaging in patriotic self-sacrifice during World War I. President Woodrow Wilson called on "The Women's Land Army of America" to reduce food consumption so that there would be more food for the troops. After all, "Food is Ammunition." An organization called the Women's Central Committee on Food Conservation assisted the effort by publishing a cookbook with patriotic recipes that used substitutes for the meat, wheat, fats, sugar, and milk needed by fighting men. The authors explained that "All the blood, all the heroism, all the money and munitions in the world will not win this war unless our [troops] . . . are fed."[11] Meanwhile, political leaders and public commentators urged wives and mothers to sacrifice full-time domesticity in order to play a larger role in economic production for the war effort. Women's cooperation at home and their production in defense industries broadcast their patriotism and bolstered suffragists' argument that women ought to be seen as contributors to the public good, not dangers to public order.

Woman's struggle for citizenship gradually gained support but also generated a backlash based on reinvigorated fears of disorderly women. Antifeminist critics attacked suffragists for selfishness, sexual perversity and promiscuity, and family abandonment. They condemned working wives for emasculating their husbands and weakening men's sense of family responsibility. They blamed working mothers for child neglect and subsequent juvenile criminality. Some critics even denounced traditional female domesticity and household management because women appeared to be using their homes to create mini-matriarchal empires. Alas, women were greedy and malicious. The moral of most antifeminist stories was that women ought to be governed by men rather than stir up public disorder by claiming equal rights to men.

American women finally won the national right to vote with the ratification of the Nineteenth Amendment in 1920. They gained the civic dignity associated with voting rights and widespread recognition as deserving citizens. Nevertheless, women's suffrage did not automatically result in major changes in women's private or public lives. Husbands and fathers still exercised patriarchal rule over women within families. Moreover, women's political rights remained significantly truncated. For example, many voting women continued to be excluded from jury pools. Finally, women's participation in elections did not produce a higher tone of public discourse or more compassionate laws and policies. As Judith Shklar puts it, "When women finally went to the polls, it turned out to be the biggest non-event in our electoral history."[12]

What did change, gradually but significantly, was women's economic opportunities and activities. Especially in the 1940s and 1950s, growing numbers of American women, including married women and mothers, moved into the wage labor force. Once there, they were commonly segregated into female job categories such as secretary or elementary school teacher. They received significantly lower pay than men for doing comparable work. And they were systematically excluded from promotion into higher-paying, more authoritative jobs that were reserved for men. It was many decades before women were able to use their voting rights and citizenship status to begin the process of reversing gender inequities in the marketplace. The first major political payoffs included the passage of the Equal Pay Act of 1963 and the Civil Rights Act of 1964. These laws helped to shield women from job discrimination and ensure them fairer treatment in the workplace.

The civil rights movement and the New Left student movement added impetus to the feminist politics of 1960s. Women's rights at home, women's opportunities in educational institutions, women's status in the workplace, women's depiction in popular culture, and women's representation in protest movements and mainstream politics were subjected to analysis, debate, and action. Many feminists concluded that men's patriarchal domination of women persisted both in private and public life regardless of the passage of women's suffrage and recognition of women's citizenship. Acting on this conclusion, feminists initiated and promoted a nationwide effort to pass an Equal Rights Amendment to the U.S. Constitution.

THE STRUGGLE AGAINST EQUAL RIGHTS

The main clause of the proposed Equal Rights Amendment (ERA) read: "Equality of rights under the law shall not be denied or abridged by the United States or by any other State on account of sex." The U.S. Congress approved the ERA in 1972 and, in the next year, some twenty-five state legislatures added their assent. By 1977 a total of thirty-five states had ratified the ERA. However, supporters failed to win ratification from the required thirty-eight states. Indeed, some state legislatures that initially approved the ERA voted to rescind ratification. A major reason why the battle for the ERA ultimately failed was because antifeminists mobilized an influential opposition by reviving and reinvoking the founders' gendered legacy.

Phyllis Schlafly led opposition to the ERA. Her book, *The Power of the Positive Woman*, presented oppositional thinking as a twentieth-century update of the founders' doctrine of republican womanhood.[13] Schlafly emphasized that the sexes were born different. In particular, "The female body with its baby-producing organs" was designed for motherhood. Women had a God-given, natural right to motherhood. Unfortunately, women were not free to exercise their right to motherhood and experience the joys of motherhood unless husbands and fathers fulfilled their natural responsibility to provision, protect, and preside over their families.

Schlafly argued that wives' dependence on their husbands and subordination to them actually benefited women and penalized men. If women complained about diapers and dishes as a "never-ending, repetitious routine," they needed to remember that men who worked to support their families generally held jobs that were "just as repetitious, tiresome, and boring." If women complained about "servitude to a husband," they needed to be reminded that their husbands' "servitude to a boss" was far less tolerable. All in all, female domesticity offered human rewards that included freedom from the marketplace, the intimacy between a mother and child, and the virtue associated with raising good citizens. By contrast, men's family responsibilities and economic servitude tended to be unending and alienating. Domestic women were far better off than their patriarchal husbands.

Schlafly asserted that most women agreed with her analysis. They had long consented to a traditional, patriarchal division of family labor. Indeed, "marriage and motherhood have always been the number-one career choice of the large majority of women." Even with suffrage, women tended to cast their votes to protect their legal right to be "full-time wives and mothers" by insisting on their husbands' legal responsibility to "support their wives and children." Schlafly recognized that many mothers were forced by necessity to perform wage labor outside of their homes. Nonetheless, she argued, working mothers maintained a sort of domestic consciousness: "When a mother combines two careers, she remains the psychological parent . . . who always feels a direct personal responsibility for the whereabouts and feelings of each child." Women's domesticity was deepseated and undeniable.

Women's domesticity also was the decisive factor in determining women's place in public life. Schlafly argued that women should remain anchored to family life but inspire their husbands and sons to behave morally, protect their family interests, and promote patriotism in politics. The founders' doctrine of republican womanhood, which enjoined domestic women to teach men to practice civic virtue and good citizenship, was alive and well among the ERA opposition. Schlafly added that married women should feel free to take advantage of their flexible household schedules and their leisure (born of time-saving appliances) to engage in practical politics to help preserve and protect their families. She had no objection to women participating in local petitioning, organizing, lobbying, and voting so long as they remembered that their families always came first and their families were the foremost focus of their political activities.

Schlafly's main quarrel with the ERA was that the amendment would have destroyed patriarchal family life and public order. For her, equal rights meant that women would no longer be able to count on the courts to require men to provision and protect their families. Without these legal guarantees, more and more women would suffer men's financial abandonment. They would be forced to support themselves and their children. Additionally, women would be liable to being drafted into military service. The ERA would make life more nasty and brutish for mothers and children.

Schlafly also feared that the ideology of equality at the foundation of the ERA invited women to reject family life, take up full-time careers, and fight for political rights in local and national arenas. More American women were likely to become "public women" who upset conventional patterns of civility and codes of deference that protected public order. Even worse, the rhetoric and reality of equal rights would free men from family responsibilities, divorce them from the civilizing influence of domestic women, and thereby invite them to vent their destructive passions, impulses, and interests in evermore chaotic and violent ways. All in all, the ERA opposition concluded, equal rights was a recipe for public disaster.[14]

The ERA died in 1982—but the contest over the founders' gendered legacy continues. Should women claim moral superiority and political power on the basis of their traditional association with domesticity, their capacity for motherhood, and the promise that they are likely to foster greater compassion and integrity than men? Or should women simply demand equal rights, equal pay, and equal political influence in a nation where they continue to suffer physical abuse at home, wage discrimination in the workplace, and underrepresentation in local, state, and national politics? Moreover, as women come to play more prominent roles in the economy and politics, are they likely to forsake family life, refuse responsibility for civilizing men, and contribute to crime and other forms of public disorder? Yesterday's questions remain relevant to today's politics.

THE DURABLE FAMILY MAN

Americans have not pushed for an Equal Rights Amendment for men. The main reason is that once excluded and subordinated men have made numerous successful attempts to achieve full citizenship. For example, poor whites, former slaves, and Asian immigrants all overcame major obstacles to attain civil and political rights. Simultaneously, however, American elites responded to popular demands for greater inclusiveness by reinforcing the traditional male hierarchies that stigmatized disorderly men, provided limited influence to married men, and afforded great authority to leaders. Generation after generation of American boys adapted to these male hierarchies and generation after generation of American men participated in them.

Like America's eighteenth-century sons of liberty, America's nineteenth-century boys established pecking orders among themselves. The most successful boys displayed considerable independence in anticipation of manhood. Middle-status boys earned a modest place in the pecking order by exhibiting exuberance and displaying disdain for adult authority. Boys who lacked proper size, appearance, intelligence, or athletic skills often had to fight for respect. Those boys who lost these confrontations or ran away from them were likely to be stigmatized and humiliated, often by being treated as girls or by being associated with girls.

This stigma continued to adhere to marginal adult men such as bachelors of age. An 1848 magazine article reported, "The unmarried man is looked upon with distrust. He has no abiding place, no anchor to hold him fast, but is a mere piece of float-wood on the great tide of time." An 1850 novel entitled *Reveries of a Bachelor* criticized single men for their reluctance to assume the manly obligations of marriage. Pre–Civil War magazines and novels castigated bachelors as disorderly creatures who desired freedom without responsibility. Post-war frontier towns became magnets for irresponsible single males who were a major source of social chaos and bloody violence. Writers urged bachelors to discipline desire, marry good women, and contribute to public order.[15]

Nineteenth-century reformers sought to monitor male sexuality and moral conduct. Advocates of "social purity" identified immigrant men with delinquency, promiscuity, obscenity, and alcohol. They demanded that all young men marry and establish a patriarchal division of labor in their families. Reformers saw traditional marriages as the main means to get disorderly young males to devote themselves to family life, act morally and responsibly, and support and govern their wives and children. Those men who failed to conform to standards of middle-class manhood were stigmatized and sometimes labeled as "namby-pamby, goody-goody gentlemen" or "impotent sissies." Such verbal assaults figured into elites' effort to maintain control of low-status, disorderly males.[16]

Most observers agreed that family men were more likely than bachelors to behave in an orderly, law-abiding manner. The *New York Post* explained, "The only way to make husbands sober and industrious [is] to keep women dependent on them." Responsible for supporting a dependent wife, a husband had a strong incentive to work steadily and reliably. He forced himself to "man" the work benches, shops, factories, and offices where he was subjected to further discipline by his bosses and managers. Employers usually saw the family man as a comparatively trustworthy employee and gave him preference in hiring and promotions. Bankers often considered him a comparatively good risk and gave him access to credit. Economic leaders advised enterprising male youths, "If you are in business, get married, for the married man has his mind fixed on his business and his family and is more likely of success."[17]

At the beginning of the twentieth century, German sociologist Werner Sombart noticed that marriage had a pacifying effect on American men and on American politics. He suggested that American workers' family commitments insulated them against personal misconduct and distanced them from political excess. Sombart calculated that American workers spent more of their time and income on family interests, were generally more contented with their lives, and deferred more regularly to public authorities than German workers, who spent more time and money on personal vices and exhibited stronger tendencies toward social discontent and political subversion.[18]

Of course, American elites opposed subversive politics. They feared that impoverished men, distraught farmers, labor militants, and recent immigrants were overwhelming the nation by making and supporting radical social and political demands that imperiled public order. National elites launched a campaign to persuade Americans to strive for conformist middle-class Protestant family life as the foundation for national prosperity and public peace. Edward Bok of the *Ladies' Home Journal* instructed his readers to celebrate and appreciate matrimony: "If young men got married, they would be more likely to get and hold a respectable job." Ellen Richards, a leader in the new domestic sciences, urged women to get their husbands more deeply involved in family life, assume responsibilities of home ownership and career development, and raise virtuous sons to be responsible, law-abiding citizens. And Theodore Roosevelt resurrected the founders' familiar solution to male disorders when he asserted: "No man can be a good citizen who is not a good husband and a good father."[19]

ENDURING ELITES

The more that the diverse ranks of American family men were admitted to citizenship, the more that national elites demanded the authority to control and govern them. Andrew Jackson was among the first presidents to understand that political elites could most effectively rule common citizens not by using brute force or by proclaiming gentlemen's superiority but by cultivating public affection. Jackson and his followers constantly curried public favor. They praised average family men. They proclaimed that farmers and frontiersmen were blessed with natural grace and wisdom. They applauded the common man's fortitude and the militiaman's courage. And they honored citizens' liberty and virtue as the mainsprings of national prosperity and democratic politics. Heaping praise upon the common man, Jackson and his supporters solicited popular consent, ultimately, to the authority of powerful national leaders.

Jacksonians felt that powerful national leaders were needed to govern the savagery (symbolized by Creek Indians) and snobbery (associated with European aristocrats) that often characterized common men's attitudes and behavior. Jackson presented himself as a great leader who avoided the unmanly extremes of savagery and snobbery. Instead, he was "nature's nobleman." He exemplified America's pioneering spirit elevated by refinement. He tempered his rugged bearing with civility. He was a simple man and citizen who happened to command extraordinary leadership abilities. Jackson deployed this mixed imagery of nature and nobility along with compassion and patriotism to claim great presidential prerogative and maintain public support. Opponents' accused him of acting like a "military chieftain" but with little effect.

During the Civil War, Abraham Lincoln became an extremely powerful political leader in two senses. First, he played the part of a stern but affectionate father figure—Father Abraham—who ruled the national family, resanctified it, called for filial sacrifice, sought the redemption of the South, and brought forth the rebirth of the nation. Lincoln conveyed the public image of a great hero, a "re-founding father," who could be trusted with extraordinary authority. Second, Lincoln was a Jacksonian man of action who, in the midst of crisis, showed little regard for legal restraints and procedural nicities. He declared martial law, suspended *habeas corpus*, centralized power, used soldiers to suppress dissent, and allowed generals such as Sherman and Grant to ignore international law by waging total war against the South. Like many founders, Lincoln felt that great patriarchal leaders did whatever they thought necessary to resolve immediate crises and secure the nation's future.

Post–Civil War America punctuated a prolonged period of peace with profound public conflict. Were emancipated slaves to be admitted to full citizenship? Did European and Asian immigrants imperil the dominion of white Protestants? Would the battle of the sexes escalate into a long-term war of attrition? Did militant unionists and socialist activists threaten private property and national security? Elites worried that the United States could not withstand so much diversity and divisiveness. Accordingly, they gradually transformed Lincoln's model of powerful leadership into a permanent fixture of American politics. The stage was set for progressive statesmen such as Woodrow Wilson and activist presidents such as Franklin Delano Roosevelt to devalue the democratic participation of common men and demand instead an active state administered by powerful national elites.

Whenever juvenile delinquency or mob actions appeared to threaten public order, these powerful national elites questioned the ordinary family man's sense of responsibility and the average family's ability to produce new generations of virtuous, law-abiding citizens. Civic leaders reacted to family failings by establishing and expanding public institutions such as almshouses, orphanages, reformatories, asylums, and penitentiaries to manage "rehabilitative regimens of order, industry, and proper family life." Ideally, these public institutions would transform delinquent boys into "practical men of business and good citizens in the middle class of society." Similarly, leaders promoted public schooling as a means to provide a disciplined, educated workforce for the economy and a stable, law-abiding citizenry for the nation. Educator Horace Mann announced that a major function of public schools was to teach boys "to moderate their passions and develop their virtues." American leaders came to rely on public institutions to rehabilitate disorderly males and promote public order.[20]

By the early twentieth century, judges increasingly functioned as "public custodians of the family." The emergence of domestic-relations law and family courts indicated growing judicial regulation of young people's sexuality, courtship, marriage, parental and reproductive rights and responsibilities, child care, divorce, and custody disputes. Sociologist George Eliot Howard articulated the main rationale for judicial oversight: "In no part of the whole range of human activity is there such imperative need of state interference and control as in the sphere of matrimonial relations. . . . The highest individual liberty can be secured only when it is subordinated to the highest social good." Domestic-relations judges became "new kinds of patriarchs" who compensated for family men's flaws and ruled the private lives of men, women, and children in the service of peace, prosperity, and good citizenship.[21]

Overall, national elites promoted penal institutions, welfare agencies, public schools, and family courts to teach responsibility to boys and reform men. However, they did not forsake coercion as an important means to procure public order. During the 1894 railroad strikes, for example, officials called out 32,000 militiamen and 16,000 regular troops to force an end to the strikes. A few years later, national elites endorsed a proposal to require all young men to undergo "universal military training" in order to learn obedience and patriotism. General Leonard Wood argued that mandatory military training would lower crime rates, raise productivity, and produce "a much higher type of citizenship."[22] Wood wanted all American males to be quiescent, law-abiding citizens who deferred to powerful political leaders.

TODAY'S "NEW MAN"?

A recent sociological study suggests that today's boys still "tend to be overtly hierarchical." They "mark rank" by exhibiting admired qualities as well as by issuing "insults, direct commands, challenges, and threats." High-status boys seek respect and deference. Middle-status boys jockey for position. Low-status boys suffer humiliation. We can see polar extremes in the following contrast: "John, who was the tallest boy in the class and one of the best athletes in the school, deftly handled challenges to his authority. Dennis, who was not very good at sports or at academics, was at the other end of the pecking order. John . . . called Dennis 'Dumbo' and insulted him in other ways." These boys grow into men who continue to build hierarchies and "compete with each other . . . for the differential payoffs that patriarchy allows men."[23]

Why do American men recreate and perpetuate hierarchies? Many modern, high-status American males still have traditional patriarchal sensibilities. They see themselves as independent men and manly leaders who protect dependent, subordinate women, especially from other dangerous males. These self-styled male authorities are "sure of their own goodheartedness and wisdom" but remain fearful of other men's "exploitative efforts."[24] To the extent that many of today's high-status males agree with the founders that most men are disorderly creatures, they locate themselves among the social and political elites they consider sufficiently wise, virtuous, and trustworthy to govern common men and all women.

Low-status males have strong incentives to consent to the very hierarchies that subordinate them. Mark Gerzon observes that the average American male is fearful that other men will treat him "as a boy and not a man." Powerful men play on this fear to control other men. Historically, white males reinforced their domination of black and Indian males by labeling them children and treating them as dependents. Why should any modern man care if the powerful treat him like a boy? One reason may be that many males harbor "fears of being humiliated . . . by other men." Another reason is that humiliation often is a forerunner to more substantial punishments, such as exclusion from discourse, decision making, and benefits. The safest strategy for low-status males seeking to avoid shame and punitive sanctions is to adhere to the dominant standards of manhood in the hope of achieving at least a modest respectability in the male pecking order.[25]

The main route to modest respectability in the male pecking order has not changed significantly since the founding era. It still involves establishing individual independence, assuming family responsibility, and governing subordinates. Enduring norms of manhood declare that males ought to be independent-minded breadwinners who earn sufficient wealth to settle down, marry, sire children, make family decisions, and perpetuate family dynasties. Periodically, this declaration is reaffirmed by social critics who first complain that bachelorhood is causing family decline, social breakdown, and political disarray and who then call on American men to recommit themselves to family responsibility and civic order. Today, liberals and conservatives alike criticize American men for failing to commit themselves to family life. They advocate a revival of "family values" to encourage men to rebuild the family nest and raise new generations of civic-minded citizens.

Americans witnessed two major attempts to redefine the meaning of male respectability in the 1960s and 1970s. One involved the efforts of college students to relocate male independence from economic self-sufficiency and family life to personal growth and political engagement. In 1962 a group known as Students for a Democratic Society issued a manifesto that called on young men to strive for personal authenticity and creativity rather than material gain and conformity. Student activists promoted "participatory democracy" and criticized "the power elite." For nearly ten years, they fought for "student power" and "people power" against the elite "Establishment" that controlled universities, manufactured destructive weapons, and sponsored the Vietnam War.

The student protest movement disappeared in the early 1970s but its demands for male authenticity and more democracy persisted. Meanwhile, millions of women, seniors, gay people, disabled Americans, and others demanded their fair share of political influence. They took part in a "backyard revolution" that involved organizing, deliberating, and asserting ordinary people's power in local political arenas. The argument that average men and women should exercise greater control in public life challenged the authority of governing elites—and generated a traditional, patriarchal backlash. Critics of backyard rebels claimed that an "excess of democracy" was causing disorder in American public life.

A second attempt to redefine the meaning of male respectability was initiated in the early 1970s by a small movement committed to the notion that "men's liberation" required an end to patriarchy. Men especially needed to be liberated from the crippling physical and mental stress associated with the breadwinner role. Liberation would enable them to lead longer, healthier lives. Moreover, men in search of personal meaning and fulfillment needed to build egalitarian relationships with the strong, independent women who were emerging from the feminist movement. Warren Farrell's best-selling book, *The Liberated Man*, listed twenty-one reasons why men would benefit if they gave up their patriarchal privileges and promoted greater sexual equality.[26]

The men's movement hoped to make the meaning of manhood more flexible. The traditional model of manhood was flawed. But instead of offering up a single model to replace it, men's activists and men's studies scholars announced that there were many and varied "masculinities." These masculinities encompassed a male productivity ethic but also a male parenting ethic. They included competitive norms but also cooperative norms. Overall, the men's movement criticized patriarchy as damaging to men and promoted a flexible pro-feminist politics that persists today, for example, in the National Organization of Men Against Sexism (NOMAS) and kindred groups. Not surprisingly, the pro-feminist men's movement generated a backlash among Americans who wanted men to resume their traditional role as responsible family patriarchs. In the 1990s a conservative Christian coalition called Promise Keepers generated widespread public support by calling on men to return to their God-given role as family providers, protectors, and potentates.

The founders' gendered legacy continues to be contested in an ongoing debate over the meaning of manhood and politics. Will males continue to create hierarchies among themselves to perpetuate weak citizenship and elite leadership? Or will they begin to reshape personal relationships and public power along more participatory and democratic lines? Will respectable manhood remain focused on independence, family, and governing dependents? Or will a "new man" emerge who strives for authenticity, seeks out strong women, and joins them in opposition to patriarchy? Will new ideals of manhood remain symbolic rhetoric or will they have a tangible impact on male behavior? Like the founders, modern national leaders who believe human beings are fundamentally flawed creatures are unlikely to support freeing women from the constraints of domesticity or freeing men to practice participatory citizenship.

TOWARD GENDER EQUALITY

The American founders' gendered legacy persists into the twenty-first century. It is particularly evident in political leaders' tendency to privilege problems associated with disorderly men and to privilege solutions proposed by elite men. Women's voices in American politics remain relatively subdued while most men's preferences in American politics are subordinated to the priorities of the male elites who still dominate political decision making.

Today's leaders associate the nation's major political problems with domestic crime and international conflict. The main perpetrators of public disorder and violence in both arenas are males. The overwhelming majority of rapists, thieves, and murderers are male. The most notorious terrorists and death-dealing dictators are male. To the extent American politics centers on protecting citizens' life, liberty, and property from male threats of disorder and violence, American elites give top priority to controlling male misconduct at home and resisting it abroad.

This priority tends to perpetuate patriarchal politics. The more citizens feel that they must rely on politicians to protect them, the more politicians are able to centralize power. This centralizing tendency is manifested in law enforcement practices that sacrifice people's civil liberties in the name of investigating, apprehending, charging, convicting, and imprisoning male suspects. This centralizing tendency is especially manifested in foreign policy where the American public has little say, less knowledge, and very few checks on elite decision making.

Additionally, the more that citizens feel dependent on government to protect them against male disorders, the greater the likelihood that citizens will elect politicians who promise to "get tough" with the bad guys. This "get tough" politics almost always favors male candidates over female candidates and produces the kind of politicians who first declare war on crime and international criminals and then appropriate vast public resources for more prisons and new weapon systems. Important issues such as domestic abuse, reproductive rights, or the feminization of poverty get comparatively little consideration and even fewer public resources.

The practice of privileging males as the main problems and main problem-solvers in American politics *may* now be weakening. To the extent that more women have become perpetrators of crime and violence, both at home and abroad, women have gained greater recognition as political problems and priorities. To the degree that more women have become police officers and soldiers as well as prosecutors, judges, ambassadors, representatives, senators, and now a Secretary of State, they have won greater recognition as political problem-solvers. For worse and for better, when women become fifty percent of the problem and fifty percent of the problem-solvers, we will have made significant progress toward gender equality in American politics.

I find it quite astonishing that the founders' gendered legacy of neglecting women in public life and privileging elite men in politics has been so resilient. The founders' legacy has survived the founding era, outlasted the establishment of women's suffrage, and continued beyond the admission of most adult males to citizenship. The fact that the founders' gendering of American politics persists today is as remarkable as it is regrettable.

Notes

CHAPTER 1

1. Linda K. Kerber, *Toward an Intellectual History of Women* (Chapel Hill: University of North Carolina Press, 1997), 129; *see also* 264–67.

2. Benjamin Franklin, "Reply to a Piece of Advice," in J. A. Leon Lemay, ed., *Writings* (New York: Library of America, 1987), 249–50.

3. Kenneth Lockridge, *On the Sources of Patriarchal Rage: The Commonplace Books of William Byrd and Thomas Jefferson and the Gendering of Power in the Eighteenth Century* (New York: New York University Press, 1992), 60.

4. Thomas Paine, "American Crisis III," in Philip S. Foner, ed., *The Life and Major Writings of Thomas Paine* (New York: Citadel Press, 1961), 90.

5. Samuel McClintock, "A Sermon on Occasion of the Commencement of the New Hampshire Constitution," in Ellis Sandoz, ed., *Political Sermons of the American Founding Era, 1730–1805* (Indianapolis: Liberty Press, 1991), 800.

6. Carole Pateman, *The Sexual Contract* (Stanford: Stanford University Press, 1988), ch. 1.

7. John Adams to James Sullivan, May 26, 1776, in Alpheus Thomas Mason and Gordon E. Baker, eds., *Free Government in the*

Making: Readings in American Political Thought, 4th ed. (New York: Oxford University Press, 1985), 120.

    8. Theophilus Parsons, "The Essex Result," in Charles S. Hyneman and Donald S. Lutz, eds., *American Political Writings during the Founding Era, 1760–1805* (Indianapolis: Liberty Press, 1983), 1:497.

    9. Royall Tyler, "The Contrast, A Comedy in Five Acts," in Paul Lauter, gen. ed., *The Heath Anthology of American Literature*, 2d ed. (Lexington, MA: D. C. Heath, 1994), 1:1108–09.

    10. Jay Fliegelman, *Declaring Independence: Jefferson, Natural Language, and the Culture of Performance* (Stanford: Stanford University Press, 1993), 130; Glenna Matthews, *The Rise of Public Woman: Woman's Power and Woman's Place in the United States, 1630–1970* (New York: Oxford University Press, 1992), chs. 1–2.

    11. Thomas Jefferson to James Madison, February 14, 1783, in James Morton Smith, ed., *The Republic of Letters: The Correspondence between Thomas Jefferson and James Madison, 1776–1826* (New York: Norton, 1995), 1:223; Jefferson to Madison, December 16, 1786, in Ibid., 1:459; Jefferson to Madison, June 20, 1787, in Ibid., 1:481; Thomas Jefferson, "Autobiography," in Merrill D. Peterson, ed., *Writings* (New York: Library of America, 1984), 92–93; Jefferson to Charles Bellini, September 30, 1785, in Ibid., 833; Jefferson to Anne Willing Bingham, February 7, 1787, in Ibid., 888; Jefferson to Bingham, May 11, 1788, in Ibid., 923; Jefferson to George Washington, December 4, 1788, in Ibid., 932–33.

    12. Jefferson to Anne Willing Bingham, May 11, 1788, in *Writings*, 922–23.

    13. Jefferson, "Notes on the State of Virginia," in Merrill D. Peterson, ed., *The Portable Thomas Jefferson* (New York: Viking Press, 1975), 96–98.

    14. Joy Day Buel and Richard Buel, Jr., *The Way of Duty: A Woman and Her Family in Revolutionary America* (New York: Norton, 1984), 66.

    15. Adams to Sullivan, May 26, 1776, in *Free Government*, 120–21.

CHAPTER 2

    1. Jefferson quoting Thomas Otway's *The Orphan*, in Lockridge, *On the Sources of Patriarchal Rage*, 60.

2. Judith Sargent Murray, "On the Equality of the Sexes," in Sharon M. Harris, ed., *Selected Writings of Judith Sargent Murray* (New York: Oxford University Press, 1995), 12–13.

3. Stephanie Coontz, *The Social Origins of Private Life: A History of American Families 1600–1900* (London: Verso, 1988), 147.

4. Anonymous, "Verses Written by a Young Lady, On Women Born to be Controll'd," in *The Heath Anthology*, 1:701–2; "Journal of Grace Growden Galloway," in Ruth Barnes Moynihan, Cynthia Russett, and Laurie Crumpacker, eds., *Second to None: A Documentary History of American Women* (Lincoln: University of Nebraska Press, 1993), 1:173.

5. Annis Boudinot Stockton to Julia Stockton Rush, March 22, 1793, in Carla Mulford, ed., *Only for the Eye of a Friend: The Poems of Annis Boudinot Stockton* (Charlottesville: University Press of Virginia, 1995), 305–06; Mercy Otis Warren, "Conscious Dignity that Ought Rather to be Cherish'd," in *Second to None*, 1:170.

6. Murray, "On the Equality of the Sexes," in *Selected Writings*, 7; Anonymous, "Impromptu, on Reading an Essay on Education, By a Lady," in *The Heath Anthology*, 1:704; Warren, "Conscious Dignity," in *Second to None*, 1:170.

7. John Adams to Abigail Adams, April 14, 1776, in *Free Government*, 119–20.

8. Murray, "Observations on Female Abilities," in *Selected Writings*, 38–41; "Desultory Thought upon the Utility of Encouraging a Degree of Self-Complacency, Especially in Female Bosoms," in Ibid., 46, 48.

9. Benjamin Franklin, "The Autobiography," in L. Jesse Lemisch, ed., *The Autobiography and Other Writings* (New York: New American Library, 1961), 157; Milcah Martha Moore, "The Female Patriots. Address'd to the Daughters of Liberty in America," in *The Heath Anthology*, 1:683; Abigail Adams to John Adams, October 20, 1777, in Charles Francis Adams, ed., *Familiar Letters of John Adams and His Wife Abigail Adams during the Revolution* (Freeport, NY: Books for Libraries Press, 1970), 317; Jonathan Mayhew, "The Snare Broken," in *Political Sermons*, 248; George Duffield, "A Sermon Preached on a Day of Thanksgiving," in Ibid., 779.

10. Paine, "American Crisis I," in *The Life and Major Writings*, 51, 57; Murray, "Observations on Female Abilities," in *Selected Writings*, 17–29.

11. Noah Webster, "On the Education of Youth in America," in Frederick Rudolph, ed., *Essays on Education in the Early Republic* (Cambridge: Harvard University, 1965), 69.

12. Washington to Eleanor Parke Custis, January 16, 1795, in Thomas J. Fleming, ed., *Affectionately Yours, George Washington: A Self-Portrait in Letters of Friendship* (New York: Norton, 1967), 244.

13. Stockton, "Lucinda and Aminta, a pastoral on the capture of Lord Cornwallis and the British army, by General Washington," in *Only for the Eye of a Friend*, 111; "The Vision," in Ibid., 177; Murray, "Observations on Female Abilities," in *Selected Writings*, 38.

14. Murray, "On the Equality of the Sexes," in *Selected Writings*, 4; "Desultory Thoughts," in Ibid., 46–47.

15. Murray, "On the Equality of the Sexes," in Ibid., 4–5, 7; Samuel Wales, "The Dangers of Our National Prosperity; and the Way to Avoid Them," in *Political Sermons*, 853.

16. Stockton to Julia Stockton Rush, March 22, 1793, in *Only for the Eye of a Friend*, 305.

17. Murray, "Observations on Female Abilities," in *Selected Writings*, 42.

18. Stockton to Julia Stockton Rush, March 22, 1793, in *Only for the Eye of a Friend*, 305.

19. Abigail Adams to John Adams, August 14, 1776, in *Familiar Letters*, 213; David Ramsay, *The History of the American Revolution* (Indianapolis: Liberty Press, 1990), 2:496–97.

20. Stockton, "Impromptu on reading several motions made against Mr. Hamilton," in *Only for the Eye of a Friend*, 174; Washington to Annis Boudinot Stockton, August 31, 1788, in Ibid., 216–17.

21. Hannah Webster Foster, *The Coquette*, in Carla Mulford, ed., *The Power of Sympathy and The Coquette* (New York: Penguin, 1996), 139.

22. Judith Sargent Murray, *The Gleaner* (Schenectady, NY: Union College Press, 1992), appendix to the 1798 ed.

23. Joseph Lathrop, "A Miscellaneous Collection of Original Pieces," in *American Political Writings*, 1:662; Washington to Stockton, August 31, 1788, in *Only for the Eye of a Friend*, 216–17.

24. Thomas Paine, "An Occasional Letter on the Female Sex," in Michael S. Kimmel and Thomas F. Mosmiller, eds., *Against the Tide: Pro-Feminist Men in the United States, 1776–1990: A Documentary History* (Boston: Beacon, 1992), 63–66; Abigail Adams to John Adams, March 31, 1776, in *Familiar Letters*, 148–50.

25. James Wilson, "Lectures on Law," in James DeWitt Andrews, ed., *The Works of James Wilson* (Chicago: Callaghan and Co., 1896), 1:29–31.

26. Kerber, *Toward an Intellectual History of Women*, 297.

27. Tara Church, my brilliant undergraduate research assistant, makes this argument.

28. John Dickinson, "Observations on the Constitutions Proposed by the Federal Convention VIII," in Bernard Bailyn, ed., *The Debate on the Constitution: Federalist and Antifederalist Speeches, Articles and Letters during the Struggle over Ratification* (New York: Library of America, 1993), 2:427.

29. Abigail Adams to John Adams, May 9, 1776, in *Familiar Letters*, 170.

CHAPTER 3

1. Susanna Rowson, *Charlotte Temple: A Tale of Truth* (New York: Penguin, 1991), 1.

2. Bridget Richardson Fletcher, "Hymn LXX, the Duty of Man and Wife," in *The Heath Anthology*, 1:663.

3. "Matrimonial Republican" quoted in Sara M. Evans, *Born for Liberty: A History of Women in America* (New York: Free Press, 1989), 63.

4. Benjamin Rush, *My Dearest Julia: The Love Letters of Dr. Benjamin Rush* (New York: Neale Watson Academic Publications, 1979), 6, 20–21; Alexander Hamilton to Elizabeth Hamilton, July 13, 1781, in Alexander Hamilton, *A Biography in His Own Words*, Mary-Jo Kline, ed. (New York: Harper and Row, 1973), 98; Franklin, "Rules and Maxims for Promoting Matrimonial Happiness," in *Writings*, 152; Franklin to John Alleyne, August 9, 1768, in Ibid., 836–37.

5. Maxine L. Margolis, *Mothers and Such: Views of American Women and Why They Changed* (Berkeley: University of California Press, 1984), 26–27, 30.

6. Joan Hoff, *Law, Gender, and Injustice: A Legal History of U.S. Women* (New York: New York University Press, 1991), 117–18.

7. Mercy Otis Warren to Winslow Warren, December 24, 1779, in Edmund M. Hayes, "Mercy Otis Warren versus Lord Chesterfield, 1779," *William and Mary Quarterly*, 3d series, 40:4 (October 1983): 620; William Hill Brown, *The Power of Sympathy*, in *The Power of Sympathy and The Coquette*, 29.

8. Stockton to Julia Stockton Rush, March 22, 1793, in *Only for the Eye of a Friend*, 306.

9. P. W. Jackson quoted in Kerber, *Toward an Intellectual History of Women*, 38–39.

10. Alice Izard to Margaret Manigault, May 29, 1801, in *Second to None*, 1:202.

11. Brown, *The Power of Sympathy*, 25–27.

12. Joanna Bowen Gillespie, "1795: Martha Laurens Ramsay's 'Dark Night of the Soul,' " *William and Mary Quarterly*, 3d series, 48:1 (January 1991): 68; John Adams to Abigail Adams, August 11, 1777, in *Familiar Letters*, 290.

13. Mercy Otis Warren, *History of the Rise, Progress and Termination of the American Revolution, interspersed with Biographical, Political and Moral Observations*, Lester H. Cohen, ed. (Indianapolis: Liberty Press, 1988), 1:xli-xliii.

14. Murray, "Observations on Female Abilities," in *Selected Writings*, 29, 36.

15. Benjamin Rush, "A Plan for the Establishment of Public Schools and Diffusion of Knowledge in Pennsylvania, to which are Added, Thoughts upon the Mode of Education, Proper in a Republic, Addressed to the Legislature and Citizens of the State," and "Thoughts Upon Female Education, Accommodated to the Present State of Society, Manners, and Government in the United States of America," in *Essays on Education*, 22, 28, 36.

16. Ibid., 22; Webster, "On the Education of Youth in America," in Ibid., 68–69.

17. Noah Webster, "An Oration on the Anniversary of the Declaration of Independence," in *American Political Writings*, 2:1239;

Ramsay, *The History of the American Revolution*, 2:496–97; Linda K. Kerber, *Women of the Republic: Intellect and Ideology in Revolutionary America* (Chapel Hill: University of North Carolina Press, 1980), 230; Simeon Doggett, "A Discourse on Education," in *Essays on Education*, 159.

18. Joyce Appleby, *Liberalism and Republicanism in the Historical Imagination* (Cambridge: Harvard University Press, 1992), 29.

19. Kerber, *Women of the Republic*, 199–200.

20. Jan Lewis, "The Republican Wife: Virtue and Seduction in the Early Republic," *William and Mary Quarterly*, 3d series, 44 (October 1987): 720; Murray, "On the Equality of the Sexes," in *Selected Writings*, 11.

21. Carol Berkin, *First Generations: Women in Colonial America* (New York: Hill and Wang, 1996), 199.

CHAPTER 4

1. George Washington, "The Rules of Civility and Decent Behavior in Company and Conversation," in George Washington, *George Washington: A Collection*, W. B. Allen, ed. (Indianapolis: Liberty Press, 1988), 6–13; "Farewell Orders to the Armies of the United States, November 2, 1783," in Ibid., 268–69.

2. Mayhew, "The Snare Broken," in *Political Sermons*, 241, 249.

3. Franklin, "Celia Single," in *Writings*, 189–90.

4. John Adams to Abigail Adams, July 7, 1774, in *Familiar Letters*, 20; George Washington, "General Orders, July 10, 1776," in Ralph K. Andrist, ed., George Washington, *A Biography in His Own Words* (New York: Harper and Row, 1972), 153.

5. John Adams to John Taylor, in George Peek, ed., *The Political Writings of John Adams* (Indianapolis: Bobbs-Merrill, 1954), 206.

6. Samuel Adams quoted in Kerber, *Women of the Republic*, 31; Samuel Williams, "The Natural and Civil History of Vermont," in *American Political Writings*, 2:956.

7. Samuel Adams quoted in A. J. Langguth, *Patriots: The Men Who Started the American Revolution* (New York: Simon and Schuster, 1988), 98; Moses Mather, "America's Appeal to the Impartial World," in *Political Sermons*, 483; Ramsay, *The History of the American Revolution*, 1:183; Warren, *History of the Rise, Progress and Termination of the American Revolution*, 1:212; Simeon Howard, "A

Sermon Preached to the Ancient and Honorable Artillery Company in Boston," in *American Political Writings*, 1:205.

8. Carroll Smith-Rosenberg, "Dis-Covering the Subject of the 'Great Constitutonal Discussion,' 1786–1789," *Journal of American History* 79:3 (December 1990): 849, 854–56.

9. William Bradford, "An Enquiry How Far the Punishment of Death is Necessary in Pennsylvania," in *Reform of Criminal Law in Pennsylvania: Selected Inquiries, 1787–1819* (New York: Arno Press Reprint, 1972), 29.

10. Franklin, "Poor Richard's Almanac," in *Writings*, 1233, 1283.

11. Ramsay, *The History of the American Revolution*, 1:23; Jefferson, "Notes on the State of Virginia" in *The Portable Thomas Jefferson*, 214–215.

12. Samuel Walker, *Popular Justice: A History of American Criminal Justice* (New York: Oxford University Press, 1980), 15, 24; Raymond A. Mohl, "Poverty, Pauperism, and Social Order in the Preindustrial American City, 1780–1840," in Joseph M. Hawes, ed., *Law and Order in American History* (Port Washington, NY: Kennkat Press, 1979), 31–32.

13. Hamilton, "On Marriage," in *A Biography in His Own Words*, 17; Murray, *The Gleaner*, 309–312.

14. Franklin, "Rules and Maxims for Promoting Matrimonial Happiness," in *Writings*, 152.

15. Fisher Ames, "Address to the Massachussets Ratifying Convention," in *The Debate on the Constitution*, 1:894–95.

16. Michael Meranze, *Laboratories of Virtue: Punishment, Revolution, and Authority in Philadelphia, 1760–1835* (Chapel Hill: University of North Carolina Press, 1996), 69–70.

17. Benjamin Rush, "An Enquiry into the Effects of Public Punishments upon Criminals and Upon Society," in *Reform of Criminal Law in Pennsylvania*, 4, 8, 10, 14; Samuel Quarrier to Thomas Jefferson, February 13, 1802, in Jack McLaughlin, ed., *To His Excellency Thomas Jefferson; Letters to a President* (New York: Avon Books, 1991), 150.

18. Meranze, *Laboratories of Virtue*, 177–79, 184–85; *Pennsylvania Gazette*, September 26, 1787, in Negley K. Teeters, *The Cradle of*

the *Penitentiary: The Walnut Street Jail at Philadelphia, 1773–1835* (Philadelphia: Pennsylvania Prison Society, 1955), 132.

19. Bradford, "An Enquiry," in *Reform of Criminal Law*, 7.

CHAPTER 5

1. John Adams, "Discourses on Davila," in *The Political Writings*, 176–77, 192; Warren, *History of the Rise, Progress and Termination of the American Revolution*, 1:3; Paine, "American Crisis," in *The Life and Major Writings*, 52–53; "Brutus X," in *The Debate on the Constitution*, 2:88.

2. Duffield, "A Sermon Preached on a Day of Thanksgiving," in *Political Sermons*, 784–85; William Emerson, "An Oration in Commemoration of the Anniversary of American Independence," in Ibid., 1568.

3. Jefferson to Frances Hopkinson, March 13, 1789, in *Writings*, 942.

4. Simeon Baldwin, "Oration at New Haven, Connecticut, July 4, 1788," in *The Debate on the Constitution*, 2:516–18, 523.

5. Hamilton, "Address to the New York Ratifying Convention," in *The Debate on the Constitution*, 2:770–771; Robert R. Livingston, "Address to the New York Ratifying Convention," in Ibid., 2:778–79.

6. Melancton Smith, "Address to the New York Ratifying Convention," in *The Debate on the Constitution*, 2:760–62; "From the 'Federal Farmer' to the 'Republican,' " in Ibid., 1:260; "Brutus III," in Ibid., 1:321; Samuel Bryan, "Centinel I," in Ibid., 1:53; "An Officer of the Late Continental Army," in Ibid., 1:103; Luther Martin, "The Genuine Information I," in Ibid., 1:638.

7. Anonymous, "A Revolution Effected by Good Sense and Deliberation," in *The Debate on the Constitution*, 1:13; Webster, "A Citizen of America," in Ibid., 1:162; Thomas B. Wait to George Thatcher, January 8, 1788, in Ibid., 1: 727; Bryan, "Centinel II," in Ibid., 1:78–79; Bryan, "Centinel VIII," in Ibid., 1:688.

8. Tunis Wortman, "A Solemn Address to Christians and Patriots," in *Political Sermons*, 1519; Jefferson to John Adams, October 28, 1813, in *The Portable Thomas Jefferson*, 534; Jefferson to George Washington, April 16, 1784, in Ibid., 368–369.

9. Henry St. John Bolingbroke, "The Idea of a Patriot King," in *The Works of Lord Bolingbroke* (Philadelphia: Carey and Hart, 1841), 2:374, 377, 391–92, 395–97, 401, 407, 419, 422–23, 426, 428.

10. Gad Hitchcock, "An Election Sermon," in *American Political Writings*, 1:299; Phillips Payson, "A Sermon," in Ibid., 1:537; Samuel Cooper, "A Sermon on the Day of the Commencement of the Constitution," in *Political Sermons*, 643, 652–53; Samuel McClintock, "A Sermon on Occasion of the Commencement of the New Hampshire Constitution," in Ibid., 802, 806–07; Samuel Langdon, "The Republic of the Israelites as Example to the American States," in Ibid., 959, 965; Israel Evans, "A Sermon Delivered at the Annual Election," in Ibid., 1070; Timothy Stone, "An Election Sermon," in *American Political Writings*, 2:846, 854; Murray, "Sketches of the Present Situation in America," in *Selected Writings*, 66; Peres Fobes, "An Election Sermon," in *American Political Writings*, 2:996.

11. James Wilson, "Address to the Pennsylvania Ratifying Convention," in *The Debate on the Constitution*, 1:825; Zephaniah Swift Moore, "An Oration on the Anniversary of the Independence of the United States of America," in *American Political Writings*, 2:1214; Alexander Addison, "Analysis of the Report of the Committee of the Virginia Assembly," in Ibid., 2:1063; Henry Holcombe, "A Sermon Occasioned by the Death of Washington," in *Political Sermons*, 1409–11.

12. Stanley Griswold, "Overcoming Evil with Good," in *Political Sermons*, 1551–52.

13. John Tucker, "An Election Sermon," in *American Political Writings*, 1:167; Hitchcock, "An Election Sermon," in Ibid., 1: 293.

14. Wales, "The Dangers of our National Prosperity," in *Political Sermons*, 851; John Mitchell Mason, "The Voice of Warning to Christians," in Ibid., 1451–52; Patrick Henry, "Speeches," in Ralph Ketcham, ed., *The Anti-Federalist Papers and the Constitutional Convention Debates* (New York: New American Library, 1986), 200; Fobes, "An Election Sermon," in *American Political Writings*, 2:998; Jeremiah Atwater, "A Sermon," in Ibid., 2:1183; Fisher Ames, "The Dangers of American Liberty," in Ibid., 2:1320.

15. Webster, "An Oration on the Anniversary of the Declaration of Independence," in *American Political Writings*, 2:1231.

16. George Washington to Bushrod Washington, September 30, 1786, in *George Washington: A Collection*, 335–36; Joel Barlow, "A

Letter to the National Convention," in *American Political Writings*, 2:832; Roger Sherman, "Congressional Debates," in Helen E. Veit, Kenneth R. Bowling, and Charlene Bangs Bickford, eds., *Creating the Bill of Rights: The Documentary Record from the First Federal Congress* (Baltimore: Johns Hopkins University Press, 1991), 151.

17. Jeremiah Wadsworth, "Congressional Debates," in *Creating the Bill of Rights*, 156; Hamilton, Federalist No. 71, in Alexander Hamilton, James Madison, and John Jay, *The Federalist Papers*, Clinton Rossiter, ed. (New York: New American Library, 1961), 432.

18. Washington to Joseph Reed, July 4, 1780, in *George Washington: A Collection*, 150–51; Madison to Jefferson, June 2, 1780, in *The Republic of Letters*, 1:140.

19. Katherine Auspitz, "Civic Virtue: Interested and Disinterested Citizens," in Edward C. Banfield, ed., *Civility and Citizenship in Liberal Democratic Societies* (New York: Paragon House, 1992), 19; Hamilton to Elizabeth Hamilton, July 13, 1781, in Hamilton, *A Biography in His Own Words*, 98.

20. Jefferson to John Colvin, September 10, 1810, in Ralph Ketcham, *Presidents Above Party: The First American Presidency, 1789–1829* (Chapel Hill: University of North Carolina Press, 1984), 172; Jefferson to John Breckinridge, August 12, 1803, in Thomas Jefferson, *Jefferson Himself: The Personal Narrative of a Many-Sided American*, Bernard Mayo, ed. (Charlottesville: University Press of Virginia, 1970), 250.

21. Washington to Alexander Hamilton, October 29, 1795, in *George Washington: A Collection*, 615; Hamilton to Edward Carrington, May 26, 1792, in *Free Government*, 309.

22. Edmund Randolph in *The Anti-Federalist Papers and the Constitutional Convention Debates*, 69.

23. Madison, Federalist No. 40, 252–55; Federalist No. 43, 279.

24. Madison to Edmund Randolph, January 10, 1788, in Michael Kammen, ed., *The Origins of the American Constitution: A Documentary History* (New York: Penguin, 1986), 97.

25. Hamilton, Federalist No. 34, 207.

CHAPTER 6

1. Murray, "Sketch of the Present Situation in America," in *Selected Writings*, 53–56, 62–66.

2. John Stevens, Jr., "Americanus V," in *The Debate on the Constitution*, 1:492–93.

3. Paine, "Common Sense," in *The Life and Major Writings*, 17; "American Crisis II," in Ibid., 69; "An Officer of the Late Continental Army," in *The Debate on the Constitution*, 1:104.

4. Howard, "A Sermon Preached to the Ancient and Honorable Artillery Company in Boston," in *American Political Writings*, 1:202; The Preceptor, "Social Duties of the Political Kind," in Ibid., 1:180; George Mason, "Opposition to a Unitary Executive," in *The Anti-Federalist Papers and the Constitutional Convention Debates*, 47.

5. John Adams to Abigail Adams, February 21, 1777, in *Familiar Letters*, 248.

6. Webster, "An Oration on the Anniversary of the Declaration of Independence," in *American Political Writings*, 2:1237–38; Washington to David Stuart, December 30, 1798, in *A Biography in His Own Words*, 399–400.

7. Franklin, "On Constancy," in *Writings*, 225–26; Franklin to John Alleyne, August 9, 1768, in Ibid., 836–37; "Information to Those Who would Remove to America," in Ibid., p. 979.

8. Jefferson to Edmund Pendleton, August 26, 1776, in *The Portable Thomas Jefferson*, 356–57; Mason quoted in James Madison's "Notes from the Constitutional Convention," in *The Anti-Federalist Papers and the Constitutional Convention Debates*, 147.

9. Franklin quoted in Madison's "Notes from the Constitutional Convention," in *The Anti-Federalist Papers and the Constitutional Convention Debates*, 152.

10. John Jay, Federalist No. 64, 395; James Iredell, "Address to the North Carolina Ratifying Convention," in *The Debate on the Constitution*, 2:866; Hamilton, Federalist No. 29, 186; Zachariah Johnston, "Address to the Virginia Ratifying Convention," in *The Debate on the Constitution*, 2:752, 754.

11. Hamilton, "Address to the New York Ratifying Convention," in *The Debate on the Constitution*, 2:835; James Wilson, "Address to the Pennsylvania Ratifying Convention," in Ibid., 1:825.

12. Washington to John Jay, August 15, 1786, in *George Washington: A Collection*, 333; Washington, "Farewell Orders," in Ibid.,

268–69; Hamilton, "Treasury Department Instructions, June 4, 1791," in Hamilton, *A Biography in His Own Words*, 247.

13. Franklin, "Proposals Relating to the Education of Youth in Pennsylvania," in *Writings*, 342; "A Letter from Father Abraham," in Ibid., 513–14; "Poor Richard's Almanac," in Ibid., 1281; "The Autobiography," 72–74, 104, 112–113; Jefferson to Thomas Jefferson Randolph, November 24, 1808, in *The Portable Thomas Jefferson*, 512–14; Jefferson to John Saunderson, August 31, 1820, in *Jefferson Himself*, 7; Jefferson to Charles Bellini, September 30, 1785, in Ibid., 113.

14. *United States Magazine* quoted in *Declaring Independence*, 112–113; Richard Bushman, *The Refinement of America: Persons, Houses, Cities* (New York: Random House, 1992), xix, 29, 63, 182.

15. Bushman, *The Refinement of America*, 43, 84, 411; The Preceptor, "Social Duties," in *American Political Writings*, 1:178–79; John Perkins, "Theory of Agency," in Ibid., 1:145; Adams, "Thoughts on Government," in *The Political Writings*, 91.

16. Jefferson to Edward Rutledge, June 24, 1797, in *Jefferson Himself*, 210.

17. Samuel Miller, "A Sermon on the Anniversary of the Independence of America, July 4, 1793," in *Political Sermons*, 1157; Washington to Alexander Hamilton, October 3, 1788, in *Affectionately Yours*, 213; Washington to James Craik, September 8, 1789, in Ibid., 223; Hamilton to James McHenry, January 27–February 11, 1798, in *A Biography in His Own Words*, 358; Edmund Randolph to the Virginia Legislature, October 10, 1787," in *The Debate on the Constitution*, 1:597; Stevens, "Americanus VII," in Ibid., 2:58.

18. Gordon S. Wood, *The Radicalism of the American Revolution* (New York: Knopf, 1992), 180.

19. Madison, Federalist No. 10, 82–83; Franklin, "Poor Richard's Almanac," in *Writings*, 1290; Hamilton, Federalist No. 68, 414; Adams, "Thoughts on Government," in *Free Government*, 143; Elizur Goodrich, "The Principles of Civil Union and Happiness Considered and Recommended," in *Political Sermons*, 919–920; Moore, "An Oration on the Anniversary of the Independence of the United States of America," in *American Political Writings*, 2:1217; Zabdiel Adams, "An Election Sermon," in Ibid., 1:552; Webster, "An Ora-

tion on the Anniversary of the Declaration of Independence," in Ibid., 2:1229.

20. Atwater, "A Sermon," in *American Political Writings*, 2:1178; Wood, *The Radicalism of the American Revolution*, 58, 71, 194–95; Landon Carter to George Washington, October 1776, in *Declaring Independence*, 109; Wales, "The Dangers of Our National Prosperity," in *Political Sermons*, 851; Webster, "An Oration on the Anniversary of the Declaration of Independence," in *American Political Writings*, 2:1233, 1237; Webster, "The Revolution in France," in *Political Sermons*, 1280.

21. Mary Beth Norton, *Founding Mothers and Fathers: Gendered Power and the Forming of American Society* (New York: Knopf, 1996), 207, 210; Martin Howard, Jr., "A Letter from a Gentleman at Halifax," in Bernard Bailyn, ed., *Pamphlets of the American Revolution, 1750–1776* (Cambridge: Harvard University Press, 1965), 1:542; Jefferson to Abigail Adams, November 1786, in John Adams, Abigail Adams, and Thomas Jefferson, *The Adams-Jefferson Letters: The Complete Correspondence Between Thomas Jefferson and Abigail and John Adams*, Lester J. Cappon, ed. (Chapel Hill: University of North Carolina Press, 1959), 1:157; Abigail Adams to Thomas Jefferson, August 8, 1904, in Ibid., 276–77.

22. Washington to Lund Washington, September 30, 1776, in *Affectionately Yours*, 93; Theophilus Parsons, "The Essex Result," in *American Political Writings*, 1:503–504, 519.

23. An Impartial Citizen, "A Dissertation," in *American Political Writings*, 2:1168; Franklin to George Whatley, May 23, 1785, in *Writings*, 1105; Franklin to George Washington, March 5, 1780, in Ibid., 1019; Murray quoted in "Introduction," in *Selected Writings*, xliii.

24. Charles Pinckney, "Qualifications for Suffrage," in *The Anti-Federalist Papers and the Constitutional Convention Debates*, 149; Webster, "An Oration on the Anniversary of the Declaration of Independence," in *American Political Writing*, 2:1223; Pelatiah Webster, "A Citizen of Philadelphia," in *The Debate on the Constitution*, 1:181; Annis Boudinot Stockton, "The Vision, an Ode to Washington," in *The Heath Anthology*, 1:679.

25. Paine, "American Crisis," in *The Life and Major Writings*, 51; Murray, "Observations on Female Abilities," in *Selected Writings*, 18, 23–24, 28.

26. Buel and Buel, *The Way of Duty*, 241; Nathanael Emmons, "The Dignity of Man," in *Political Sermons*, 907; Ramsay, *The History of the American Revolution*, 2:630.

27. Stevens, "Americanus V," in *The Debate on the Constitution*, 1:492–93.

28. Jefferson to John Adams, October 28, 1813, in *The Portable Thomas Jefferson*, 534; Adams, "A Defence of the Constitutions," in *The Political Writings*, 135–37.

29. Jefferson to John Adams, February 7, 1786, in *The Adams-Jefferson Letters*, 1:119; Jefferson to John Adams, November 13, 1787, in Ibid., 1:211.

30. Madison, Federalist No. 10, 82–83; Federalist No. 40, 253–54; Edmund Randolph, "Address to the Virginia Ratifying Convention," in *The Debate on the Constitution*, 2:717.

31. Madison, Federalist No. 57, 352; Hamilton, Federalist No. 35, 214–216.

CHAPTER 7

1. Frances B. Cogan, *All-American Girl: The Ideal of Real Womanhood in Mid-Nineteenth-Century America* (Athens: University of Georgia Press, 1989), 4.

2. Nancy F. Cott, "Passionlessness: An Interpretation of Victorian Sexual Ideology, 1790–1850," in Nancy F. Cott and Elizabeth H. Pleck, eds., *A Heritage of Her Own: Toward a New Social History of American Women* (New York: Simon and Schuster, 1979), 168–69.

3. Margolis, *Mothers and Such*, 30; John Demos, *Past, Present, and Personal: The Family and the Life Course in American History* (New York: Oxford University Press, 1986), 58.

4. Cogan, *All-American Girl*, 81, 89; Catherine Beecher excerpted in Jeanne Boydston, Mary Kelley, and Anne Margolis, eds., *The Limits of Sisterhood: The Beecher Sisters on Women's Rights and Woman's Sphere* (Chapel Hill: University of North Carolina Press, 1988), 127–139.

5. Karen J. Blair, *The Clubwoman as Feminist: True Womanhood Redefined, 1868–1914* (New York: Holmes and Meier, 1980), 18, 28.

6. Coontz, *The Social Origins of Private Life*, 190, 267, 330; Steven J. Ross, *Workers on the Edge: Work, Leisure, and Politics in Indus-

trializing Cincinnati, 1788–1890 (New York: Columbia University Press, 1985), 103, 169–170, 228; Caroll D. Wright quoted in Daniel Horowitz, *The Morality of Spending: Attitudes toward the Consumer Society in America, 1875–1940* (Baltimore: Johns Hopkins University Press, 1985), 18.

7. Carroll Smith-Rosenberg, "Beauty, the Beast, and the Militant Woman: A Case Study of Sex Roles and Social Stress in Jacksonian America," in *A Heritage of Her Own*, 204; Blair, *The Clubwoman as Feminist*, 1, 40–42, 49, 80; Evans, *Born for Liberty*, 76, 130, 137, 142–43.

8. Mrs. A. J. Graves, "Women in America," in Nancy F. Cott, ed., *Roots of Bitterness: Documents of the Social History of American Women* (New York: Dutton, 1972), 144–45.

9. Orestes A. Brownson, "The Woman Question," in Aileen S. Kraditor, ed., *Up From the Pedestal: Selected Writings in the History of American Feminism* (Chicago: Quadrangle Books, 1968), 192.

10. Isabella Hooker excerpted in *The Limits of Sisterhood*, 202–203, 212.

11. Joanne L. Hayes, "Fare for Hard Times," *Country Living Magazine* (March 1989): 110–111, 117.

12. Judith Shklar, *American Citizenship: The Quest for Inclusion* (Cambridge: Harvard University Press, 1991), 60–61.

13. Phyllis Schlafly, *The Power of the Positive Woman* (New York: Harcourt, Brace, Jovanovich, 1977).

14. Jane J. Mansbridge, *Why We Lost the ERA* (Chicago: University of Chicago Press, 1986), 69, 86, 103–4, 110–15.

15. Coontz, *The Social Origins of Private Life*, 213, 224; Glenna Matthews, *"Just a Housewife": The Rise and Fall of Domesticity in America* (New York: Oxford University Press, 1987), 83–85; David T. Courtwright, *Violent Land: Single Men and Social Disorder from the Frontier to the Inner City* (Cambridge: Harvard University Press, 1996), chs. 3–5.

16. David G. Pugh, *Sons of Liberty: The Masculine Mind in Nineteenth-Century America* (Westport, CT: Greenwood Press, 1983), 102–4.

17. Mimi Abramovitz, *Regulating the Lives of Women: Social Welfare Policy from Colonial Times to the Present* (Boston: South End Press, 1988), 127; Anne Norton, *Alternative Americas: A Reading of Antebellum Political Culture* (Chicago: University of Chicago Press,

1986), 31; Mary P. Ryan, *Womanhood in America: From Colonial Times to the Present*, 3d ed. (New York: Franklin Watts, 1983), 146; Coontz, *The Social Origins of Private Life*, 213; Demos, *Past, Present, and Personal*, 86.

18. Werner Sombart, *Why is there no Socialism in the United States?* C. T. Husbands, ed. (White Plains, NY: M. E. Sharpe, 1976), 93–104, 106.

19. Joe L. Dubbert, *A Man's Place: Masculinity in Transition* (Englewood Cliffs, NJ: Prentice Hall, 1979), 104–5; Horowitz, *The Morality of Spending*, 84; Theodore Roosevelt quoted in Peter Filene, "The Secrets of Men's History," in Harry Brod, ed., *The Making of Masculinities: The New Men's Studies* (Boston: Allen and Unwin, 1987), 104.

20. Abramovitz, *Regulating the Lives of Women*, 159, 166; Lyman Beecher quoted in Norton, *Alternative Americas*, 78–79; Horace Mann quoted in David E. Shi, *The Simple Life: Plain Living and High Thinking in American Culture* (New York: Oxford University Press, 1985), 122.

21. Michael Grossberg, *Governing the Hearth: Law and the Family in Nineteenth-Century America* (Chapel Hill: University of North Carolina Press, 1985), xi-xii, 87, 291, 298.

22. John W. Chambers, "Conscripting for Colossus," in Peter Karsten, ed., *The Military in America: From the Colonial Era to the Present*, rev. ed. (New York: Free Press, 1986), 301; Samuel P. Huntington, *The Soldier and the State: The Theory and Politics of Civil-Military Relations* (Cambridge: Harvard University Press, 1957), 286; Leonard Wood, "Our Military History," in Walter Millis, ed., *American Military Thought* (Indianapolis: Bobbs-Merrill, 1966), 278.

23. Barrie Thorne, *Gender Play: Girls and Boys in School* (New Brunswick, NJ: Rutgers University Press, 1993), 92–93; Joseph H. Pleck, "Men's Power with Women, Other Men, and Society," in Michael S. Kimmel and Michael A. Messner, eds., *Men's Lives* (New York: Macmillan, 1989), 25; R. W. Connell, *Gender and Power: Society, the Person and Sexual Politics* (Stanford: Stanford University Press, 1987), 110.

24. William J. Goode, "Why Men Resist," in *Men's Lives*, 45, 49.

25. Mark Gerzon, *A Choice of Heroes: The Changing Face of American Manhood* (Boston: Houghton Mifflin, 1982), 43, 93; David Leverenz, *Manhood and the American Renaissance* (Ithaca: Cornell University Press, 1989), 72–73.

26. Warren Farrell, *The Liberated Man* (New York: Random House, 1974), ch. 10.

Bibliography

Abramovitz, Mimi. *Regulating the Lives of Women: Social Welfare Policy from Colonial Times to the Present*. Boston: South End Press, 1988.

Adams, John. *The Political Writings of John Adams*. George Peek, ed. Indianapolis: Bobbs-Merrill, 1954.

Adams, John and Abigail Adams. *Familiar Letters of John Adams and His Wife Abigail Adams during the Revolution*. Charles Francis Adams, ed. Freeport, NY: Books for Libraries Press, 1970.

Adams, John, Abigail Adams, and Thomas Jefferson. *The Adams-Jefferson Letters: The Complete Correspondence Between Thomas Jefferson and Abigail and John Adams*. Lester J. Cappon, ed. 2 vols. Chapel Hill: University of North Carolina Press, 1959.

Appleby, Joyce. *Liberalism and Republicanism in the Historical Imagination*. Cambridge: Harvard University Press, 1992.

Bailyn, Bernard, ed. *The Debate on the Constitution: Federalist and Antifederalist Speeches, Articles and Letters during the Struggle over Ratification*. 2 vols. New York: Library of America, 1993.

———. *Pamphlets of the American Revolution, 1750–1776*. 2 vols. Cambridge: Harvard University Press, 1965.

Banfield, Edward C., ed. *Civility and Citizenship in Liberal Democratic Societies.* New York: Paragon House, 1992.

Berkin, Carol. *First Generations: Women in Colonial America.* New York: Hill and Wang, 1996.

Blair, Karen J. *The Clubwoman as Feminist: True Womanhood Redefined, 1868–1914.* New York: Holmes and Meier, 1980.

Bolingbroke, Henry St. John. "The Idea of a Patriot King," in *The Works of Lord Bolingbroke.* 4 vols. Philadelphia: Carey and Hart, 1841.

Boydston, Jeanne, Mary Kelley, and Anne Margolis, eds. *The Limits of Sisterhood: The Beecher Sisters on Women's Rights and Woman's Sphere.* Chapel Hill: University of North Carolina Press, 1988.

Brod, Harry, ed. *The Making of Masculinities: The New Men's Studies.* Boston: Allen and Unwin, 1987.

Brown, William Hill. *The Power of Sympathy.* Carla Mulford, ed. New York: Penguin, 1996.

Buel, Joy Day and Richard Buel, Jr. *The Way of Duty: A Woman and Her Family in Revolutionary America.* New York: Norton, 1984.

Bushman, Richard. *The Refinement of America: Persons, Houses, Cities.* New York: Random House, 1992.

Cogan, Frances B. *All-American Girl: The Ideal of Real Womanhood in Mid-Nineteenth-Century America.* Athens: University of Georgia Press, 1989.

Connell, R. W. *Gender and Power: Society, the Person and Sexual Politics.* Stanford: Stanford University Press, 1987.

———. *Masculinities.* Berkeley: University of California Press, 1995.

Coontz, Stephanie. *The Social Origins of Private Life: A History of American Families 1600–1900.* London: Verso, 1988.

Cott, Nancy F., ed. *Roots of Bitterness: Documents of the Social History of American Women.* New York: Dutton, 1972.

Cott, Nancy F. and Elizabeth H. Pleck, eds. *A Heritage of Her Own: Toward a New Social History of American Women.* New York: Simon and Schuster, 1979.

Courtwright, David T. *Violent Land: Single Men and Social Disorder from the Frontier to the Inner City.* Cambridge: Harvard University Press, 1996.

Demos, John. *Past, Present, and Personal: The Family and the Life Course in American History*. New York: Oxford University Press, 1986.

Dubbert, Joe L. *A Man's Place: Masculinity in Transition*. Englewood Cliffs, NJ: Prentice Hall, 1979.

Evans, Sara M. *Born for Liberty: A History of Women in America*. New York: Free Press, 1989.

Farrell, Warren. *The Liberated Man*. New York: Random House, 1974.

Fliegelman, Jay. *Declaring Independence: Jefferson, Natural Language, and the Culture of Performance*. Stanford: Stanford University Press, 1993.

Foster, Hannah Webster. *The Coquette*. Carla Mulford, ed. New York: Penguin, 1996.

Franklin, Benjamin. *The Autobiography and Other Writings*. L. Jesse Lemisch, ed. New York: New American Library, 1961.

———. *Writings*. J. A. Leon Lemay, ed. New York: Library of America, 1987.

Gerzon, Mark. *A Choice of Heroes: The Changing Face of American Manhood*. Boston: Houghton Mifflin, 1982.

Gillespie, Joanna Bowen. "1795: Martha Laurens Ramsay's 'Dark Night of the Soul.' " *William and Mary Quarterly*, 3d series, 48:1 (January 1991): 68–92.

Greven, Philip. *The Protestant Temperament: Patterns of Child-Rearing, Religious Experience, and Self in Early America*. New York: Knopf, 1977.

Grossberg, Michael. *Governing the Hearth: Law and the Family in Nineteenth-Century America*. Chapel Hill: University of North Carolina Press, 1985.

Hamilton, Alexander. *A Biography in His Own Words*. Mary-Jo Kline, ed. New York: Harper and Row, 1973.

Hamilton, Alexander, James Madison, and John Jay. *The Federalist Papers*. Clinton Rossiter, ed. New York: New American Library, 1961.

Hawes, Joseph M., ed. *Law and Order in American History*. Port Washington, NY: Kennkat Press, 1979.

Hayes, Edmund M. "Mercy Otis Warren versus Lord Chesterfield, 1779." *William and Mary Quarterly*, 3d series, 40:4 (October 1983): 616–21.

Hayes, Joanne L. "Fare for Hard Times." *Country Living Magazine* (March 1989): 110–111, 117.

Hoff, Joan. *Law, Gender, and Injustice: A Legal History of U.S. Women.* New York: New York University Press, 1991.

Horowitz, Daniel. *The Morality of Spending: Attitudes toward the Consumer Society in America, 1875–1940.* Baltimore: Johns Hopkins University Press, 1985.

Huntington, Samuel P. *The Soldier and the State: The Theory and Politics of Civil-Military Relations.* Cambridge: Harvard University Press, 1957.

Hyneman, Charles S. and Donald S. Lutz, eds. *American Political Writings during the Founding Era, 1760–1805.* 2 vols. Indianapolis: Liberty Press, 1983.

Jefferson, Thomas. *Jefferson Himself: The Personal Narrative of a Many-Sided American.* Bernard Mayo, ed. Charlottesville: University Press of Virginia, 1970.

———. *The Portable Thomas Jefferson.* Merrill D. Peterson, ed. New York: Viking Press, 1975.

———. *The Republic of Letters: The Correspondence between Thomas Jefferson and James Madison, 1776–1826.* James Morton Smith, ed. 3 vols. New York: Norton, 1995.

———. *Writings.* Merrill D. Peterson, ed. New York: Library of America, 1984.

Juster, Susan. *Disorderly Women: Sexual Politics and Evangelicalism in Revolutionary New England.* Ithaca: Cornell University Press, 1994.

Kammen, Michael, ed. *The Origins of the American Constitution: A Documentary History.* New York: Penguin, 1986.

Kann, Mark E. *On the Man Question: Gender and Civic Virtue in America.* Philadelphia: Temple University Press, 1991.

———. *A Republic of Men: The American Founders, Gendered Language, and Patriarchal Politics.* New York: New York University Press, 1998.

Karsten, Peter, ed. *The Military in America: From the Colonial Era to the Present.* New York: Free Press, 1986.

Kerber, Linda K. *Toward an Intellectual History of Women.* Chapel Hill: University of North Carolina Press, 1997.

————. *Women of the Republic: Intellect and Ideology in Revolutionary America*. Chapel Hill: University of North Carolina Press, 1980.

Ketcham, Ralph, ed. *The Anti-Federalist Papers and the Constitutional Convention Debates*. New York: New American Library, 1986.

————. *Presidents Above Party: The First American Presidency, 1789–1829*. Chapel Hill: University of North Carolina Press, 1984.

Kimmel, Michael S. *Manhood in America: A Cultural History*. New York: Free Press, 1996.

Kimmel, Michael S. and Michael Messner, eds. *Men's Lives*. New York: Macmillan, 1989.

Kraditor, Aileen S., ed. *Up From the Pedestal: Selected Writings in the History of American Feminism*. Chicago: Quadrangle Books, 1968.

Langguth, A. J. *Patriots: The Men Who Started the American Revolution*. New York: Simon and Schuster, 1988.

Lauter, Paul, gen. ed. *The Heath Anthology of American Literature*. 2d ed. 2 vols. Lexington, MA: D. C. Heath, 1994.

Leverenz, David. *Manhood and the American Renaissance*. Ithaca: Cornell University Press, 1989.

Lewis, Jan. "The Republican Wife: Virtue and Seduction in the Early Republic." *William and Mary Quarterly*, 3d series, 44 (October 1987): 689–721.

Lockridge, Kenneth. *On the Sources of Patriarchal Rage: The Commonplace Books of William Byrd and Thomas Jefferson and the Gendering of Power in the Eighteenth Century*. New York: New York University Press, 1992.

Madison, James. *A Biography in His Own Words*. Merrill D. Peterson, ed. New York: Harper and Row, 1974.

Mansbridge, Jane J. *Why We Lost the ERA*. Chicago: University of Chicago Press, 1986.

Margolis, Maxine L. *Mothers and Such: Views of American Women and Why They Changed*. Berkeley: University of California Press, 1984.

Mason, Alpheus Thomas and Gordon E. Baker, eds. *Free Government in the Making: Readings in American Political Thought*. 4th ed. New York: Oxford University Press, 1985.

Matthews, Glenna. *"Just a Housewife": The Rise and Fall of Domestic-
    ity in America*. New York: Oxford University Press, 1987.
————. *The Rise of Public Woman: Woman's Power and Woman's
    Place in the United States, 1630–1970*. New York: Oxford
    University Press, 1992.
McLaughlin, Jack, ed. *To His Excellency Thomas Jefferson; Letters to a
    President*. New York: Avon Books, 1991.
Meranze, Michael. *Laboratories of Virtue: Punishment, Revolution,
    and Authority in Philadelphia, 1760–1835*. Chapel Hill:
    University of North Carolina Press, 1996.
Millis, Walter, ed. *American Military Thought*. Indianapolis: Bobbs-
    Merrill, 1966.
Moynihan, Ruth Barnes, Cynthia Russett, and Laurie Crumpacker,
    eds. *Second to None: A Documentary History of American
    Women*. 2 vols. Lincoln: University of Nebraska Press, 1993.
Murray, Judith Sargent. *The Gleaner*. Schenectady, NY: Union Col-
    lege Press, 1992.
————. *Selected Writings of Judith Sargent Murray*. Sharon M. Har-
    ris, ed. New York: Oxford University Press, 1995.
Norton, Anne. *Alternative Americas: A Reading of Antebellum Po-
    litical Culture*. Chicago: University of Chicago Press, 1986.
————. *Republic of Signs: Liberal Theory and American Popular Cul-
    ture*. Chicago: University of Chicago Press, 1993.
Norton, Mary Beth. *Founding Mothers and Fathers: Gendered Power
    and the Forming of American Society*. New York: Knopf,
    1996.
————. *Liberty's Daughters: The Revolutionary Experience of Ameri-
    can Women, 1750–1800*. Boston: Little Brown, 1980.
Paine, Thomas. "An Occasional Letter on the Female Sex," in
    *Against the Tide: Pro-Feminist Men in the United States,
    1776–1990: A Documentary History*. Michael S. Kimmel and
    Thomas F. Mosmiller, eds., Boston: Beacon, 1992.
————. *The Life and Major Writings of Thomas Paine*. Philip S.
    Foner, ed. New York: Citadel Press, 1961.
Pateman, Carole. *The Sexual Contract*. Stanford: Stanford University
    Press, 1988.
Pugh, David G. *Sons of Liberty: The Masculine Mind in Nineteenth-
    Century America*. Westport, CT: Greenwood Press, 1983.

Ramsay, David. *The History of the American Revolution.* 2 vols. Indianapolis: Liberty Press, 1990.

Reform of Criminal Law in Pennsylvania: Selected Inquiries, 1787–1819. New York: Arno Press Reprint, 1972.

Ross, Steven J. *Workers on the Edge: Work, Leisure, and Politics in Industrializing Cincinnati, 1788–1890.* New York: Columbia University Press, 1985.

Rotundo, E. Anthony. *American Manhood: Transformations in Masculinity from the Revolution to the Modern Era.* New York: Basic Books, 1993.

Rowson, Susanna. *Charlotte Temple: A Tale of Truth.* New York: Penguin, 1991.

Rudolph, Frederick, ed. *Essays on Education in the Early Republic.* Cambridge: Harvard University Press, 1965.

Rush, Benjamin. *My Dearest Julia: The Love Letters of Dr. Benjamin Rush.* New York: Neale Watson Academic Publications, 1979.

Ryan, Mary. *Womanhood in America: From Colonial Times to the Present.* 3d ed. New York: Franklin Watts, 1983.

Sandoz, Ellis, ed. *Political Sermons of the American Founding Era, 1730–1805.* Indianapolis: Liberty Press, 1991.

Schlafly, Phyllis. *The Power of the Positive Woman.* New York: Harcourt, Brace, Jovanovich, 1977.

Shi, David E. *The Simple Life: Plain Living and High Thinking in American Culture.* New York: Oxford University Press, 1985.

Shklar, Judith. *American Citizenship: The Quest for Inclusion.* Cambridge: Harvard University Press, 1991.

Smith-Rosenberg, Carroll. "Dis-Covering the Subject of the 'Great Constitutional Discussion,' 1786–1789." *Journal of American History* 79: 3 (December 1990): 841–73.

Sombart, Werner. *Why Is There No Socialism in the United States?* C. T. Husbands, ed. White Plains, NY: M. E. Sharpe, 1976.

Stansell, Christine. *City of Women: Sex and Class in New York: 1789–1860.* Urbana: University of Illinois Press, 1987.

Stockton, Annis Boudinot. *Only for the Eye of a Friend: The Poems of Annis Boudinot Stockton.* Carla Mulford, ed. Charlottesville: University Press of Virginia, 1995.

Teeters, Negley K. *The Cradle of the Penitentiary: The Walnut Street Jail at Philadelphia, 1773–1835.* Philadelphia: Pennsylvania Prison Society, 1955.

Thorne, Barrie. *Gender Play: Girls and Boys in School.* New Brunswick, NJ: Rutgers University Press, 1993.

Veit, Helen E., Kenneth R. Bowling, and Charlene Bangs Bickford, eds. *Creating the Bill of Rights: The Documentary Record from the First Federal Congress.* Baltimore: Johns Hopkins University Press, 1991.

Walker, Samuel. *Popular Justice: A History of American Criminal Justice.* New York: Oxford University Press, 1980.

Warren, Mercy Otis. *History of the Rise, Progress and Termination of the American Revolution, interspersed with Biographical, Political and Moral Observations.* Lester H. Cohen, ed. 2 vols. Indianapolis: Liberty Press, 1988.

Washington, George. *Affectionately Yours, George Washington: A Self-Portrait in Letters of Friendship.* Thomas J. Fleming, ed. New York: Norton, 1967.

———. *A Biography in His Own Words.* Ralph K. Andrist, ed. New York: Harper and Row, 1972.

———. *George Washington: A Collection.* W. B. Allen, ed. Indianapolis: Liberty Press, 1988.

Wilson, James. *The Works of James Wilson.* James DeWitt Andrews, ed. 2 vols. Chicago: Callaghan and Co., 1896.

Withington, Ann Fairfax. *Toward a More Perfect Union: Virtue and the Formation of American Republics.* New York: Oxford University Press, 1991.

Wood, Gordon S. *The Radicalism of the American Revolution.* New York: Knopf, 1992.

Index

Equal Rights Amendment
(ERA), 149–52
Evans, Israel, 97

Farrell, Warren, 160
Federalist Papers, 7
Federalists, 95, 98, 115
Fletcher, Bridget Richardson,
50
Fobes, Peres, 98
Foster, Hannah Webster, 41
Franklin, Benjamin, 10, 16, 18,
34, 52, 76, 79–80, 83,
95–96, 111, 117–18, 125,
130, 132
Freemasons, 19

Galloway, Grace Growden,
30
Gentleman legislators, 113–14,
127–29, 134, 136
Gentlemen, 124–27
George III, King, 105
Gerzon, Mark, 158
Gillespie, Joanna Bowen, 58
Griswold, Stanley, 99

Hamilton, Alexander, 16, 52,
83, 95, 103, 107–10, 135
Hancock, John, 41
Hawthorne, Nathaniel, 143
Henry, Patrick, 101
Hitchcock, Gad, 97
Hobbes, Thomas, 8
Hoff, Joan, 53
Hooker, Isabella, 146
Howard, George Eliot, 157
Howard, Martin, 129
Howe, William, 78

Iredell, James, 120
Izard, Alice, 56

Jackson, Andrew, 154–55
Jay, John, 120
Jefferson, Thomas, 6, 8, 16,
18–21, 25, 33–34, 62, 79,
81, 93, 96, 100, 107–8, 111,
118, 125–26, 133
Johnston, Zachariah, 120

Kerber, Linda, 5, 44

Langdon, Samuel, 97
Lathrop, Joseph, 42
Leadership, 91, 94, 97, 105,
110; and crisis, 105–10; and
mobility, 131–34; patriarchal
language of, 96–99, 110; and
political manhood, 99–105;
and political prerogative,
101–5, 108, 110, 136; and
reputation, 129–31; strong,
154–57; weak, 111, 127–29;
and women, 131–32. *See also*
Gentleman legislators; Natural aristocrats
Lewis, Jan, 65
Lincoln, Abraham, 155–56
Livingston, Robert R., 95
Locke, John, 9
Lockridge, Kenneth, 6

Madison, James, 16, 38, 106,
108–9, 118–19, 135
Manhood: and citizenship,
84–85; and crime, 85–90;
and disorder, 37–38, 62–63,
71, 75–77, 81–82, 135, 140;

About the Author

MARK E. KANN is Professor of Political Science and holds the USC Associates Chair in Social Science at the University of Southern California. He is the author of several books, including *A Republic of Men* (1998).

ISBN 0-275-96111-7

HARDCOVER BAR CODE